# TRAINING the COMMUNITY EDUCATOR

# TRAINING the COMMUNITY EDUCATOR:
# A Case-Study Approach

BY

ROBERT I. BERRIDGE          PHILIP T. WEST

STEPHEN L. STARK

PENDELL
PUBLISHING
COMPANY

International Standard Book Number:   0-87812-145-5

Library of Congress Catalog Card Number:   76-3173

# Table of Contents

# Preface

Community education is rapidly becoming a major movement in education today. In an age of isolation, alienation, restlessness, and change, it promises to each participant an opportunity to regain a sense of community. Through a variety of course offerings, participants are able to pursue academic and avocational interests and job-related skills. Through specific programs, such as those aimed at preschoolers, high school dropouts, and senior citizens, broad societal needs are met. More important, however, is the process which gives impetus to all of these activities — the democratic process, or participatory structures which bring people together to solve their most pressing problems in the best way possible.

Community education is an echo of the progressive era. It is, as well, the little red schoolhouse revisited. Functioning at an optimal level, community education has all the openness and flexibility of open education. Community education is directed toward individual interests and group harmony, and its credo is learning by doing.

The Gemeinschaft of medievalism is very much a part of community education. Like the medieval age, community education fosters a feeling of togetherness that is akin to the finest notion of family. The contemporary neighborhood is vaguely reminiscent of yesterday's fiefdom. Neighborhoods are capable of promoting belongingness and identity, as did the medieval fiefdom despite the servitude it engendered. The major difference between the fiefdom and the neighborhood is that feudal rank has been replaced by block leadership earned through effort and admiration. In medieval society each person had a place and a particular role to play. Under the processes and programs of community education, everyone belongs, all creeds, colors, and nations; and all are treated equally no matter how humble or ennobled their origins. At the moment, community education is revitalizing neighborhoods, towns, and cities. In subsequent years, it may do the same for nations as its philosophy extends the democratic process into other lands.

At its core, then, community education is synonymous with family and the community school. But the community school is merely the key to the creation of a larger family — a family of agencies, institutions, organizations, and businesses joined together to bring community members to new heights of awareness and participation.

This new familial relationship is not always easy to establish. Diverse groups, often estranged and operating, as it were, in somewhat of a vacuum, are reluctant to lose their respective identities or minimize the number or importance of their activities, however replicative they may be. The result is a redundancy of effort and a waste of physical, financial, and human resources.

Educating the greater community to the potentialities of community education takes a special brand of leadership. Only a person with vision, temerity, verve, and almost boundless energy can hope to accomplish the goals of community education. Yet the possession of these personal qualities is, in itself, no guarantee that the converts to community education will be equal to the task ahead. Training, therefore, becomes fundamental to the success of community educators, and the most effective kind of training springs directly from the insights a prospective leader can gain from the experiences of others deeply involved in the movement.

What community education will be a decade from now is difficult to determine. Presently, the emphasis is on the community school and its linkages with other community groups. With the advent of education as a lifelong process, with early retirement, increased leisure, and the necessity to retool periodically to stay abreast of technological developments, community education may take on a totally new dimension. It is, in fact, conceivable that the community school of today may become the school community of tomorrow. Much formalized learning may occur outside of the school in multiple settings, including the home.

In the home, learning may be organized under the auspices of the school community, conducted over a wall-sized television screen with a two-way communication system, and supervised by a traveling community educator. Indeed, learning centers may be housed in condominium settings, where immediate access to recreational facilities and educational television makes possible unique opportunities in community education. Inasmuch as industrial sectors will become an integral part of the school community of the future, additional community education opportunities to learn and have fun on the job are likely to emerge. And as municipalities and agencies combine with the school in a coordinating fashion heretofore unimagined, a new level of community education will be attained. In embracing all aspects of community life, the school community will embody the community education philosophy and become the byword for the advancement of learning and the improvement of society.

Armchair speculation, however, is not a panacea for dealing with the more immediate problems of community education. Before a grandiose plan can be wholeheartedly addressed, community educators must be equipped to resolve a myriad of contemporary problems. Out of the resolution of these problems, it is hoped that the opportunities of tomorrow will be forged.

For many years case studies have been used with considerable success in the training programs of educators. Case studies re-create a reality which may be vicariously experienced by trainees in classroom settings. Indeed, using case studies, novice and veteran alike may test or improve their decision-making skills. Freed from stress and strain or inexperience, which might have caused others to err judgmentally, trainees are encouraged to apply their skills to a variety of common or unique problem situations.

Believing that the case study is one of the most effective ways to share insights and sharpen skills, the authors have selectively combined ten years of field experiences into a single textbook of twenty-four cases. Deriving its empirical basis from the implementation and operation of community education projects in at least one hundred communities, the text is specifically designed to train community education personnel.

Despite its anonymity, each case presented in the text has resulted from an experience gleaned from field work. Situations typify experiences daily encountered by community education leaders.

The text may be used as a tool to develop conceptual, technical, and human relations skills in higher education preparatory programs and in inservice workshop training sessions.

Eight topical areas are covered in the text: awareness, planning, staffing, coordinating, policy-making, financing, leadership, evaluation. By participating in the questions and related activities accompanying each case, the student will be afforded an opportunity to become an effective community education leader. A list of suggested annotated readings complement and enrich the text, offering to students additional opportunities to broaden their knowledge and appreciation of the community education movement.

In closing this introductory statement, it is perhaps appropriate to add that the authors contributed equally and laboriously to the development of this text, mirroring the first tenet of community education — cooperation at its ultimate.

# CHAPTER 1 Creating Community Awareness

A high level of community education awareness on the part of administrators and staff within agencies, organizations and institutions, and on the part of the community in general is essential prior to the development of a community education project. The awareness phase, as defined by the authors, includes promotion, interpretation, public relations, and the community survey. Despite the fact that the survey could be included in a later chapter, it is placed here because it is the outstanding tool for obtaining awareness in the community.

Awareness is essential in the development of an all-encompassing project; and the key to awareness is the interpretation of the community education concept.

Typically, but not always, public school officials are initiators of community education. After investigating and studying the feasibility of the concept, the initiator moves to promote and interpret what community education is and how it can work. At this time, leaders from all existing resource groups, agencies, and institutions within the community are called together to gain an understanding of the concept. Unless a clear interpretation of the concept is made to agency leaders, there is a possibility that community education may appear threatening to them. Agency leaders must understand that community education is a cooperative planning and operational venture, wherein no one group is subservient to another.

1

Interpretation must also be made to public school personnel, from the custodian to the top level administrator, since many activities will directly affect the school. School personnel must become an integral part of the planning team to assure cooperation for the project. Many times, the essential effort to develop in teachers an understanding of community education is not made. The results of such neglect are unnecessary everyday operating problems.

The next step in the promotion and interpretation phase is making citizens of the community aware of the concept. It is recommended that all groups, formal and informal, clubs, churches, etc., be presented with a program concerning community education. Through a question and answer period, the concept can be fully interpreted to each and every person contacted during the meetings.

The community, or door-to-door, survey is the final, though probably most important, step in the awareness stage. The purpose for conducting a survey is, of course, to determine the needs and interests of people so that programs may be initiated. The survey instrument may also be constructed to gather information concerning resource persons and to nominate members of a community council. One of the greatest benefits, however, which is derived from the entire procedure is widespread public awareness of community education. Indeed, the survey creates awareness better than any other public relations tool.

All methods of public relations are employed during the awareness phase, from personal contact to extensive use of the media. The greater the variety of methods, the greater the awareness that develops.

The three cases described in this chapter are titled "The Administration," "The Community," and "The Home." Many cases could have been written, but these three, which have been thoroughly explored, emphasize well the thrust of the chapter — awareness through promotion, interpretation, public relations, and the survey.

**CASE #1**

## THE ADMINISTRATION

It was the last week of August and the first day back to school for the Centertown teachers. They were congregated in the Centertown High School auditorium where, as usual, orientation activities began.

Superintendent Carl Bottomly, a burly man who stood well over six feet tall, finished his opening day address. Pausing only for a moment to smile graciously to the applause he received, he quickly turned the assembly over to the principals who were to dispatch assignments. Walking up the center aisle with two of his board members, he stopped to tap George Carlson on the shoulder.

While at least two dozen heads bobbed up and down to see who was the recipient of the superintendent's attention, the graying fifty year-old leader said with a slight sense of urgency in his voice, "George, I'd like to see you at the central office this afternoon. There's something important that I'd like to share with you — a special administrative project that I have in mind. Say about two o'clock."

"I'll be there," said Carlson without deliberation.

Catching up with the board members, now a few feet ahead of him, Superintendent Bottomly quickly entered into the conversation they were having, and together they left the auditorium.

For the rest of the morning and during lunch, George Carlson, Centertown High's head football and basketball coach, waited with anticipation. Born and reared in Centertown, Carlson, an all-around sportsman and an avid teacher of four classes of sophomore history, was in his fifth year of teaching and coaching. A tall, slender but solidly built young man of twenty-seven, married and the father of two children, Carlson was extremely ambitious and anxious to make good as coach, teacher and eventually administrator. With a master's degree in educational administration and administrative certification, he was ready and eager to become Centertown's next high school principal. The current principal was due for retirement in two years.

Carlson's knees were a little shaky as he walked into the small, white brick building that housed the superintendent and his staff. The thought of promotion kept crossing his mind. To Mrs. Paler, the superintendent's secretary, he said with a tremor in his voice, "Mildred, Mr. Bottomly is expecting me."

"He'll be right with you, George," responded Mrs. Paler amicably, "as soon as he gets off the phone. Wait, I think he's off now. Let me ring him. Mr. Bottomly," she spoke into the receiver, "George Carlson's here."

"Send him in," a voice squawked into her ear.

She put down the phone. "You can go in now."

As George Carlson entered the large, carpeted room, he heard Mrs. Paler say, "Give my regards to your mother."

Superintendent Bottomly stuck out a huge hand, and Carlson shook it several times.

"George," said Bottomly, sitting down behind his desk, "I'm going to get right down to business. I need your help in a project close to my heart. Have you ever heard of community education?" Bottomly leaned forward, his arms resting on his desk.

"In one of the classes I once took in my master's degree program, I learned a little about it, enough to attest to its importance." Carlson hoped he had said enough to encourage the superintendent to pick up the conversation. At this point, he wasn't at all sure whether he had his terminology correct. He kept thinking of adult education. In any case, he did not feel comfortable about elaborating upon his understanding of community education.

"I'm glad we agree," said Bottomly. "I attended a workshop this summer which put me on top of this thing. Now I want to implement the concept. So far, the board is behind me 100 percent, and I'm going to give you all the support I can, provided you're willing to coordinate the activity. How about it, George, can I count on you?"

"I'm ready to carry the ball." Carlson smiled, suddenly thinking of his college football days.

"There's only one hitch, George. Since most of this is kind of unofficial, I mean budget and all, I won't be able to reduce your teaching load until we can justify the need for this program. Once it's underway, we'll make a formal presentation to the board and create an administrative slot for you, a prelude to the principalship I know you're interested in." Bottomly dialed Mrs. Paler's number. "Mrs. Paler, would you please bring in the file on the community education workshop I attended." Staring directly at Carlson, he said, "George, there are a lot of steps that community educators recommend for initiating a project, but I think we can skip most of them. The main thing is to launch the program by September 15. I want a lot of courses on the agenda by then."

Mrs. Paler brought in the file and left without a comment.

Bottomly picked up the file and moved away from his desk, ushering Carlson to the door. "I know you've got a sizable load, coaching and teaching, but I've got faith in you, George. Take the file and give me a call if there's anything I can help you with. By the way, here are the keys to the building. You've got it made."

Carlson was intermittently elated and depressed when he left the superintendent's office. If he succeeded with the program, he was sure to earn himself a principalship. However, because of his unfamiliarity with community education, he couldn't help worrying about the possibility of failure.

That night he studied Bottomly's notes, and the following morning he made a list of evening courses he would offer. A few of his friends suggested that he make the gymnasium available for a variety of athletic endeavors. But for Carlson the idea held little merit. The gym had to be set aside for the exclusive use of the school's athletic program. Anywhere else in the high school would be fine for conducting classes.

For three weeks, Carlson worked feverishly on a brochure that would be available for distribution in the offices of all schools in the district. Listing ten courses and featuring a cadre of interested and excellent teachers, his finished product was exceptionally attractive. To gain administrative support, Carlson met with building principals to discuss his program. A few calls by Carlson to his closest friends, teachers and parents, seemed to guarantee additional support. A call to the editor of the local newspaper promised to produce for Carlson a small blurb about community education in the *Centertown Times* a week before classes began. Carlson's enthusiasm was so great that he began missing practice sessions on the high school gridiron. Having delegated the activity somewhat begrudgingly to an assistant coach named Frank Peterson, he sat behind closed doors in his coach's quarters planning for what he hoped would be an impressive turnout at registration day.

When the big day rolled around, Carlson was ready. Assisting him in the registration process were his wife and three teachers. By 9:00 p.m. on Monday, September 15, twenty-one people had registered for four of the courses: eleven in high school equivalency, six in ceramics-beginning, two in law for the layman and two in needlecraft. When registration closed at 10:00 p.m., only six more people had enrolled, two in a course called appreciation of the novel and four in auto mechanics. The courses in folk guitar and country songs and in modern mathematics did not attract any registrants.

Against his better judgment, a somewhat defeated Carlson continued the registration process for the remaining four days of the week. Although a total of thirty-two people had enrolled by Sunday, only one course was scheduled to run. This was the high school equivalency course which had fifteen registrants in it. Beginning ceramics, running second in the lineup with an apparent interest quotient of seven, was, like the others, scheduled to be scrapped. It was at this time that Carlson seriously considered giving up his community education project, for in no way could he account for the failure he had just experienced.

## QUESTIONS

1. Did Superintendent Bottomly have enough information concerning community education to initiate a project? Did he envision a community school or a community education project?

2. To what extent was George Carlson's background suited to the role of community education director? What position in the public school system is closely akin to the role of director?

3. Superintendent Bottomly's charge was to omit "the recommended steps." What strategies of developing awareness in the community were omitted?

4. Given to Carlson were a set of keys and a mandate to start programs by September 15. Is it possible to make a community aware of community education in approximately three weeks? How long is needed to acquaint and interpret community education to a community?

5. Carlson was expected to continue his coaching and teaching job on a full-time basis until the project got off the ground. Can community education be adequately promoted by a part-time coordinator? If not, how much time from his teaching and coaching duties should Carlson be given to coordinate the project?

6. The program was briefly discussed with the principals. Is an informal session sufficient to make a principal aware of community education?

7. Carlson's call to the editor of the *Centertown Times* promised to produce a small blurb in the newspaper about community education. Was this a good technique? What other public relations tools could have been utilized?

8. The brochure developed by Carlson was distributed through the school offices. How else might distribution of the brochures have been accomplished?

9. List the methods Carlson used to promote community education. Critique the effectiveness of each.

10. Since only one class made the registration quota, should the project be dropped or should the one class be taught?

## ACTIVITIES

1. Rewrite the critical phases of the case study so that there is a chance for community education to succeed.

2. Brainstorm how Carlson might have made the community aware of community education despite his three-week limitation.

3. Construct a timetable designed to make maximum use of Carlson's three weeks.

4. Role play Carlson's presentation to the building principals. How would he explain community education, his role, and the project?

5. Write the news release Carlson had asked to be printed.

6. Role play the meeting of Carlson and Bottomly following class registration.

**CASE #2**

## THE COMMUNITY

After the results of his first setback had worn off, George Carlson was ready to carry his program directly to the community. Since the most likely place to begin was among his own circle of friends, Carlson arranged to give a pep talk on community education, just one week later, to the Athletic Boosters' Club.

Everybody in Centertown who knew George Carlson admired him. This was especially true of the members of the Athletic Boosters' Club. They had gratefully watched "good ol' George" lead the football and basketball teams of Centertown to repeated victories. There were many proud fathers who waited for him to speak tonight; about what, they were not quite certain.

Carlson exuded confidence when he faced the group. They would help, he was sure; and he desperately needed help, that no one could deny. Standing behind a podium, Carlson looked distinguished in a navy blue knit suit. The cut of his hair, and the dry look it had, made him look fashionable as well. In his hand he held a briar pipe.

"Gentlemen and fellow jocks, as we are sometimes referred to in the vernacular, I come here tonight to enlist your aid in a project that I hold dear to my heart. It is a project that involves the entire community in a school-community effort that is directed toward meeting the needs and interests of almost everyone in Centertown. It is our intention at Centertown High School — in fact, we have already begun — to offer a variety of adult education courses on our campus, courses which I am sure you will enjoy and appreciate. We'll have courses in auto mechanics, law for the layman, needlework, the appreciation of the novel, and you name it, not to mention a high school equivalency program.

"Many of us have talked about getting our school to offer these kinds of courses for a long time; and now it's all being made possible. Yet to make the program a success, you must help me to make others aware of our offerings. Indeed, as I have already indicated, I welcome you to suggest courses in which you have strong interests. There is no limit to the courses we can offer as long as we can get a sufficient number of people to enroll in them.

"As some of you know, our first showing was anything but exemplary. The truth is the program hasn't yet got off the ground. I came here tonight to share my problem — and yours — with friends of like mind. Most important, however, I came to address leaders in the community, leaders who will help me lead others into the school to take advantage of what we at Centertown High have to offer. What do you say, men? Do I have your support?"

As Carlson moved from the center of the room to his seat at the other end of the head table, a flood of remarks, some irascible, compelled him to return to the podium.

Steve Dawson, the fifty year-old proprietor of the Star Hardware Store, was the loudest to speak. "Don't get me wrong, George, but I got to admit that attending high school at night just ain't my bag. To date, I've done pretty well without a high school diploma; and I don't think the future is going to make much difference in my life. High school is okay for kids, but us adults don't need it." Applause followed, soon interrupted by continued hesitations from club members.

Before Carlson could reply, the voice of Ed Cashin, Centertown's mail carrier, spoke up. "I don't want to knock your program, George; so let me say real quick-like, that, as a majority of one, I'd rather watch television. I'm bushed when I get home at night. I want to relax."

Once the voices began, all Carlson could do was listen and wait, hopefully, to discuss some of the issues which were cropping up.

Taylor Martin, the local optometrist, stood up. "It is my understanding, correct me if I'm wrong, that there will be a ten dollar course fee. Tell me where is this extra money going to go?"

An unidentified voice yelled. "It'll probably go for teacher salaries. Those teachers are always getting raises."

Dr. Malcom Curry, Centertown's favorite general practitioner, chimed in. "George, old sport, if this program of yours doesn't generate enough funds to be self-supporting, may I expect another tax increase?"

Another unidentified voice blurted out, "I wouldn't mind school so much if it wasn't all lecture and test. Who needs 'em . That kind of stuff just wears me out. Besides, you can't smoke in class either; and let's face it, I need my nicotine."

Eli Stoner, Centertown's patriarchal druggist, honed in. "George, we've got a dozen organizations now all doing the same thing. It seems to me that we're just duplicating our efforts and paying unnecessarily for our mistakes. I'm tax poor now!"

The heat of the room was becoming oppressive to Carlson. Wiping his forehead, he took a deep breath and exhaled. Then he reached for a glass of water to lubricate his parched throat.

Melvin Starkley, vice-president of the Centertown Mortgage and

Trust, stood up to be heard. "George, it is my belief that our major concern is the improvement of our vocational education program so that we can enhance our partnerships with business and industry. Let's calmly confront the issue. If a man hasn't acquired a high school education, it is not the community's fault. Furthermore, if it's courses our citizens are after, let them attend Cedar Falls Community College; it's only ten miles away. I'd like to help you, George. We all would, but it just doesn't seem practical."

Carlson took another gulp of water. Surveying his audience to detect further objections and finding none, save a murmuring voice or two, he tried to recollect as clearly as possible the issues of gravest concern. In a second he would speak to each of these issues. He was determined to leave the club tonight with the support of all of his booster friends.

Taking off his coat and loosening his tie, George began again to address his audience, this time like the leader he really was.

## QUESTIONS

1. Carlson stated that the program would meet the needs and interests of everyone in the community. How has he determined this?

2. Are the leaders in the community represented in the Athletic Boosters' Club? Typically, is this the best type of group to provide community education with leadership?

3. Carlson's attempt at public relations with the Boosters' Club backfired. What could he have done to interpret community education to the group before asking for help?

4. Had the Boosters' Club been positive, how might its members have helped to interpret community education throughout the community?

5. Why did Carlson misread the group?

6. What issues were behind the statements made by the members?

7. What was the group's image of Carlson?

8. How will Carlson respond to the questions concerning:
   How profits would be spent,

Taxes,
Vocational education,
Cedar Falls Community College?

## ACTIVITIES

1. Rewrite the last half of the case with an enthusiastic Athletic Boosters' Club.

2. As a class activity, list groups, organizations and individuals represented in the Boosters' Club. Can the club be considered a power group?

3. Working in small groups, list the types of groups, organizations, and institutions that should be contacted during the interpretation phase of community education.

4. Rewrite Carlson's speech to the Boosters' Club to make it more effective.

5. Assume Carlson paid follow-up visits to various members of the Boosters' Club. Role play his meeting with the following persons:
    Hardware store owner,
    Mail carrier,
    Optometrist,
    Druggist,
    Vice-president of Mortgage and Trust.

6. Discuss, in small groups, Carlson's next step. Should the project continue or be shelved?

7. Construct a time line showing Carlson's promotion, interpretation, and public relations phase of implementation. Construct a contrasting time line improving Carlson's plan.

CASE #3

## THE HOME

When George Carlson sadly reported the results of his abortive efforts to Superintendent Bottomly, he still had one ray of hope left. Bottomly, while obviously disappointed, tried to encourage the young athlete to forge ahead with his new idea.

"George," said Bottomly, forcing gaiety into his voice, "If you think a community survey will help, by all means try it. I'd really like to see this program fly. When do you plan to work on the survey?"

"This weekend," answered Carlson, thinking about how he seemed to be getting further and further behind in his other activities. This project is turning into a monster, he thought.

"Get back to me Monday, George. I'll be very much interested in seeing what you come up with." He paused. "Have a good weekend, George," he added.

Rummaging through a community education resource book, Carlson discovered a list of two-hundred courses he could use to assess community interest.

He stayed up till two in the morning laboring at the typewriter. At the top of the survey sheet he took care to include detailed instructions. There he indicated that all responses were to be forwarded directly to him by October 3. The questionnaire stated: Address all replies to Mr. George Carlson; Director, Community Education; Centertown High School; Centertown 78543. It was further emphasized that an early return would guarantee that an individual's choice of activities would be given full consideration. Carlson also requested that a day be selected for scheduling the chosen activities.

The next morning, after a brief phone discussion with Superintendent Bottomly, Carlson arranged to have the typed stencils run off on yellow paper, an added touch, he believed, which would attract readers.

At 2:00 p.m., Carlson traveled throughout the district, distributing to principals or school secretaries a quantity of questionnaires sufficient to meet the needs of their enrollments. Now that the operation appeared to be moving again, Carlson couldn't conceal his excitement. Back at the high school, a happy Carlson dashed from homeroom to homeroom to check on class distribution. When the three-thirty bell rang to dismiss the students, Carlson was suddenly called to the phone.

"George, I just noticed you made no provisions in your questionnaire for the senior citizenry of our little resort community. Did you have to address it to parents only? Couldn't you have elaborated a little in your introduction to encourage their input?"

"I'll modify the questionnaire this evening, sir; and if I have to hand carry it to every senior citizen in the community, I'll do it. We'll make it, I assure you." Carlson was feeling an emptiness in his stomach and a cold sweat on his brow.

"I hope so, George." The line clicked.

As Carlson prepared to leave the high school office, he received another call, this time from the principal of Sheldon Cross Elementary School.

"George," yelled Principal Sam Barkey, "what are you trying to do — sabotage my PTA?"

"What do you mean, Sam?" Carlson was bewildered. "I don't understand!"

"That business of *pick a day* on your questionnaire. What happens if all my parents pick Wednesday? Bang, there goes my PTA attendance. My PTA night is Wednesday, George."

"I don't know what to say, Sam, or what to do. Shouldn't the parents be allowed to choose?" Carlson had difficulty catching his breath. His hands trembled.

"They won't have to, George. I didn't send them out. Furthermore, I suggest you modify your questionnaire as early as possible, that is, if you want my support. Wednesday is a no-no, George."

This time Carlson was the first to break the connection. Before he did so, however, he was told that he had a call on another line.

Carlson took the call from Reverend Peterson only to discover that Thursday was considered church night for many members of the community. That put both Wednesday and Thursday in jeopardy.

Walking along the corridors with hanging head and slumped shoulders, Carlson's eyes were drawn to what was rapidly becoming a yellow heap of paper. The custodian was sweeping up the survey questionnaires. Moving aside to allow the custodian to continue his work, Carlson's eye caught a neat pile of questionnaires on Mrs. Gorvey's desk, which apparently weren't handed out.

Carlson, now incensed by the sudden turn of events, began checking homerooms for distribution. During his inspection, he was to note that seventeen rooms still contained his questionnaires. On the verge of weeping, Carlson decided to go home. In the parking lot he saw a good deal of yellow paper strewn about, questionnaires that would never reach their destination. Carlson had failed miserably. But why, he still did not know.

That afternoon little Mary Anne Tyler gave a yellow questionnaire to her father, who was too busy watching television to read it. Later, her brother Albert made a pretty yellow paper plane out of it and threw it out his upstairs bedroom window to watch it soar. The children giggled as the paper plummeted straight to the ground.

Two weeks later, while washing clothes, Mrs. Applegate removed a soggy piece of yellow paper from her son Allen's trousers and tried to read it. She couldn't.

Centertown's community education program is now no more than a figment of Superintendent Bottomly's imagination; and Carlson is happily back to teaching and coaching, no longer sure of what his administrative desires might be.

## QUESTIONS

1. What further support should Superintendent Bottomly have given Carlson?

2. Discuss Carlson's survey plan. What are its strengths and weaknesses?

3. Is it better that Carlson or a committee construct a survey instrument? If a committee is used, who should serve on it?

4. Since most people in a community have children, was it not appropriate for Carlson to address the survey instrument to "parents only?" Explain!

5. Why didn't the teachers send the survey home?

6. Carlson requested on the survey that respondents "select a day." Discuss the pros and cons of having respondents participate in the scheduling of courses.

7. What types of information might be gathered from a survey?

8. How is it possible to obtain reliable information from a survey?

9. How can lay persons assist in a community survey?

10. What types of public relations activities should accompany a survey?

## ACTIVITIES

1. Role play the meeting between Superintendent Bottomly and George Carlson.

2. Construct a community survey instrument.

3. Plan in detail the implementation of a community-wide survey. Identify a timetable, committees, participants, and surveying techniques.

4. Using a community street directory, or a school district map, lay out routes for several surveyors. How can one avoid duplicating interviews and missing others?

5. Role play an interview between a surveyor and a local citizen.

6. In small groups, discuss the advantages of surveys. What other outcomes are possible from surveys in addition to gathering data?

7. Assume you are a community education coordinator who has just received and analyzed the data from a survey. In small groups, discuss and outline your next step.

## ANNOTATED READINGS

Berridge, Robert I. *The Community Education Handbook,* Midland, Michigan: Pendell Publishing Company, 1973. Chapter I, Community Education: A Concept with Unlimited Potential; Chapter VII, The Community Survey; Chapter IX, Block Plan of Organization. The philosophy and potential of community education are discussed, along with the two elements necessary to develop an awareness of community education, a community survey, and a block plan of organization.

Burden, Larry, and Whitt, Robert L. *The Community School Principal,* Midland, Michigan: Pendell Publishing Company, 1973. Chapter VI, (pp. 175-203). The viewpoints of principals on community education are outlined in this text. The four I's of community education are discussed, and models are developed to offer the reader an insight into the nature of school-community involvement and into the school-community role of the principal. A variety of models aimed at promoting and improving school-community relations are discussed as is the total development of the community and its perceived outcomes.

Hickey, Howard W., and Van Voorhees, Curtis. *The Role of the School in Community Education,* Midland, Michigan: Pendell Publishing Company, 1969. Chapter III, Community Education: An Overview, written by Jack D. Minzey and Clarence R. Olsen. The chapter provides an overview of the community education concept by briefly highlighting a definition, general characteristics, organization, programs, staff finances, and relationships to other agencies.

Kerensky, V. M. "Correcting Some Misconceptions About Community Education," *Phi Delta Kappan,* Volume LIV, No. 3, November 1972, (pp. 158-160). As with any movement there are many misconceptions which arise. Some people feel that community education is merely a new slogan, or a gimmick, without real depth. The author clarifies this misconception and then recapitulates the community education concept by making several salient points.

Kerensky, V. M., and Melby, Ernest O. *Education II — The Social Imperative,* Midland, Michigan: Pendell Publishing Company, 1971, (pp. 157-178). This chapter treats the community school as a process-oriented vehicle and the community as the clients for its emerging product. The authors speak of the new education and the involvement of the community. This chapter outlines twelve components essential for a well-developed community education program and cites communication and involvement as crucial towards its success.

Melby, Ernest O. "Approaches to Role Change in Community Education," *Phi Delta Kappan,* Volume LIV, No. 3, November 1972, (pp. 171-172). The article revolves around the description of a "Community Education person" and his characteristics. The author describes the democratization and humanization of education for the roles of the board, the superintendent, the principal and the coordinator. The nine areas described should enable the educational leaders of the community to change the basic model of education. A flat, not a tall organization, should exist if people are to develop as individuals.

Minzey, Jack. "Community Education: An Amalgam of Many Views," *Phi Delta Kappan*, Volume LIV, No. 3, November 1972, (pp. 150-153). The author describes the rapid growth of community education over the last decade in the light of demographic and social changes which have taken place. Viewing education as a lifetime endeavor, the author discusses and illustrates the changing role of the school. A major portion of the article defines community education and program/process. The author clearly stresses a mistake made in many communities — that of using high school facilities rather than elementary school sites. This section should be reviewed carefully by all wishing to implement community education. The article closes by describing community education as a potential technique for returning participatory democracy to our country.

Minzey, Jack, and LeTarte, Clyde E. *From Program to Process*, Midland, Michigan: Pendell Publishing Company, 1972. Chapter III, (pp. 45-77). Minzey and LeTarte devote this whole section to the awareness stage of developing community education. They state that to omit those who are to be affected by community education is a violation of the precepts of community education philosophy. The authors go on to declare that community education should be done with and not to people. This attribute must be incorporated.

Seay, Maurice F., and Associates. *Community Education: A Developing Concept*, Midland, Michigan: Pendell Publishing Company, 1974, (pp. 235-257). An in-depth study of community awareness through public communication is highlighted. Supporting the study is a twenty-year trace through the literature, which is detailed for the reader with guidelines, models, and charts.

Totten, Fred. *The Power of Community Education*, Midland, Michigan: Pendell Publishing Company, 1970. Chapter II, (pp. 21-23). The author stresses the need for communication in community education. He feels there must be effective communication within the school, the community, and between school and community. Outlined are the effective steps to be taken within the school. Specific examples of the role of the director in this domain are cited.

Whitt, Robert L. *A Handbook for the Community School Director*, Midland, Michigan: Pendell Publishing Company, 1971. Chapter I, Introduction; Chapter II, Community Involvement, (pp. 65-68). Community education is described as the difference in the learning process because quality education is the final product. Involvement techniques, in general, are listed in a usable form. The director's role in the awareness stage is also discussed.

# CHAPTER 2 Planning and Implementing

The planning and implementation stage of community education varies with many communities. The success of a project is largely dependent upon the manner in which it is implemented. Many factors are involved in the initial planning of a project, the most important of which are the commitment of school and city officials, the appointment of a steering committee, and the development of a time line. Often a project is initiated without the necessary planning, and implementation is haphazard.

One of the greatest problems facing community educators today is instant programs. Many community leaders, eager to duplicate the good things happening in a neighboring community, are inclined to initiate programs too quickly. The casual observer of community education projects is frequently left with the impression that community education is just programs. While visiting several successful projects, the observer sees only programs in operation, not the foundation upon which they are based. Unaware of the scope of activities which precede program inception, the observer assumes that the nature and design of community education are the same for all districts. Indeed, there are recorded instances where whole sets of courses have been transferred to other communities by uninformed but well-meaning educators simply because they seemed to work so well. Unfortunately, transferred courses usually prove disastrous despite good intentions.

But the key question remains: what should be done first? Should programs be started immediately, or should a lengthy awareness and involvement procedure precede program development?

In the first case in this chapter, the authors describe a situation where program precedes process. This is a rather typical error made in many communities. The questions and activities following the case afford each student an opportunity to examine, in some depth, the methods used to implement community education.

In case two the appropriateness of partial community representation is seriously questioned. A lack of planning can alter the pattern of citizen participation in a community education project. Comprehensive planning should provide for community participation in all programs. The coordinator should be aware of the change potential in the community; sites should be selected so that all citizens have access to them; councils should be representative of a cross-section of the community; and the community survey should be carried to all doors. This type of planning, coupled with a process-oriented implementation phase, most assuredly enhances the widespread success of any new project. Case two concludes by suggesting that community educators strive to meet the needs and interests of all citizens, not just a select few.

Another problem which is quite common stems from the so-called successful project. The successful project may be one in which extensive planning is involved and all steps of implementation are followed. Everything appears to be fine. The community is excited, people are participating, and commitment is substantial. Suddenly, there arises the feeling that the pinnacle of success has been attained, and future growth is impeded. The third case in the chapter addresses itself to this problem.

CASE #4

## IN THE BEGINNING THERE WAS HOPE

Superintendent George Armstrong's first encounter with the community education concept came by way of a discussion with his old friend Hank Dubois, a superintendent of a rivaling school district. Enthused by what he heard, he hastily scanned a community education textbook to familiarize himself with the basic approach. Liking what he read, he visited three community education projects. What he saw excited him more than ever. Each school was a beehive of activity — education, he thought, at its very finest. Schools were lighted and bustling with happy adults, parking lots were jammed to capacity, and bulletin boards displayed a host of community-centered activities.

Eager to start a program of his own, he copied the course listings of all three schools. Back at his own office, he reduced the huge list to what he considered the five best offerings. Next, he called in Miss Finnegan, a bright, young, third-year teacher who had been quite successful as the school newspaper and yearbook advisor, and offered her the job as part-time community education director.

Miss Finnegan, always eager to put her best foot forward no matter how difficult the task, freely accepted the challenge. Together, they put the program in motion.

For several days, Miss Finnegan ran around the building in a breathless state of exhaustion, trying to sign up her peers to teach the courses scheduled for the spring. Through sheer audacity she managed to gain consent from even those who had flatly refused to become involved when first approached. Her argument was indisputable; she and the superintendent were counting upon their participation to make the program a success. Few seemed to dispute such an earnest appeal. After all, new contracts were issued in the spring. And so the program continued to gather momentum.

When enrollment day came around, at least eighteen to twenty participants enrolled in each of the classes. The program, it would appear, was an obvious success; and both the superintendent and Miss Finnegan were proud of their efforts. The teachers who were involved in the program were happy, too. They were making extra money and enjoyed their work.

Interest in the program seemed to wane somewhat about the middle of the course. Students were complaining about irrelevant lectures and a great deal of busy work. Participating faculty seemed also to be tiring of their extra stint and losing some of their original enthusiasm. Miss Finnegan was immersed in the yearbook and had little time to devote to community education.

When summer came, Miss Finnegan took a trip to Europe, where she vacationed most of her summer. After her rigorous year, she felt she had deserved no less. Superintendent Armstrong thought little of community education during the summer. Most of his working time was spent on preparing for the new school year; his free time was spent driving back and forth to his summer cottage.

Fall appeared to arrive abruptly for students, faculty, and superintendent. And in a few short weeks the community education program was to be put in motion again. This time teachers were almost impossible to find. A few of the same ones once again were cajoled into offering their services, but most were adamant in their refusal to participate. In a pinch, Miss Finnegan was forced to teach a subject herself. Two courses were automatically closed out for lack of instructional personnel.

Enrollments in the fall were down from approximately twenty to twelve students per class. Miss Finnegan blamed it on the weather, and Superintendent Armstrong concurred. The weather was indeed, bad. Armstrong was a bit sorry that he had begun the program. It seemed to be taking up too much of his time. But Miss Finnegan was as indomitable as ever.

When the ensuing spring semester began, enrollments were even worse. In fact only three of the classes carried. As a result five new courses were quickly added. Teacher recruitment was easy in this case, for the teachers were offering their favorite diversions as courses. Unfortunately, the community clientele found other diversions and only maverick courses carried. When the spring semester finished, Miss Finnegan was absolutely tired of community education. At the moment, she had only a vague idea of what she might offer next fall and no more than three teachers who were willing to continue with the program. She thought of going outside of the district for teachers, but that seemed like a lot of unnecessary toil.

Later, as she reported her dilemma to Superintendent Armstrong, she was to admit quite candidly that her observations led her to believe that no one in the district was particularly interested in community education.

In acknowledging her observations, Armstrong not only offered his sympathy, but also his own opinion. He was of a like mind. They had tried, honestly tried; but apparently the community — at least their community — was neither interested in nor ready for community education.

His concluding remark was, "If nobody wants it, what can we do?"

## QUESTIONS

1.  What justification did Superintendent Armstrong have for believing that his community was neither ready for nor interested in community education?

2.  Miss Finnegan's duties with the yearbook continued after she took charge of the community education effort. What advantage would there have been in relieving her of this, or any other, duty?

3.  Why did the project meet with immediate success and then wane?

4.  To what extent did the project described meet the criteria for community education?

5.  Mr. Armstrong, like many others, visited successful community education projects in action. Why was his project not successful?

6.  What might Miss Finnegan have done during the summer to enhance the project?

7.  What are the advantages and disadvantages of employing public school teachers to teach community education classes?

8.  What were Mr. Armstrong's reasons for starting community education?

9.  In view of the situation described in the case, was there any chance for success? Comment.

## ACTIVITIES

1.  Role play Superintendent Armstrong's meeting with Miss Finnegan when he offered her the job of community education director.

2.  Discuss with the class several philosophies inherent in the case.

3. Using a graph, chart the participation in the project. Is this typical?

4. Role play Miss Finnegan asking her peers to teach classes.

5. In small groups, list classes which might be better taught by certified teachers. List classes which could be taught by lay persons. Compare your lists.

CASE #5

### ANOTHER MAN'S PALACE

James Taylor was not unimpressed by the architectural extravagance of Vesta High School. What impressed him more, however, were the crowded, humming corridors of adults moving to and from classes. Inside the school, surrounded by so much activity, he almost forgot the cold rainy September weather that made him wish he had stayed at home.

Taylor, an assistant superintendent from a school district some fifty miles away, was visiting Vesta this Tuesday evening at the request of his superintendent and board of education. He had come to appraise Middleberg's community education program. The leaders in his district, having only recently heard of the community education concept, were extremely interested in the full-school utilization notion. Wanting very much to better serve the needs of their citizenry, they were looking to community education as a possible answer.

Before Taylor could enter the rather lavishly decorated administrative suite, he was hailed by Jeff Davis, a dapperly dressed, youthful-looking man, who was actually in his early fifties. The tall, thin community education director stretched out his arm and offered Taylor a firm handshake.

"Glad you could come, especially on a night like this. I've been looking forward to meeting you. Can't get to know a bloke very well over a telephone, can you." Davis chuckled and clicked his heels. "Shall we begin our cook's tour," he added, twirling his pen-lined mustache.

Ordinarily, Taylor was not a man to mince words. Tonight, he used them even more sparingly. He couldn't help thinking of the miserable weather that awaited him on his return home. "I'd appreciate that very much. As you know, the weather is not conducive to driving tonight, and it could get worse."

"I assume you've read the literature I sent you about our program." Davis twirled his mustache again.

"I read it very carefully, despite the fact that I had about one hundred other things to do, all of them pressing." Taylor finished with a loud laugh. A highly respected leader in a predominantly black community,

Taylor was well-known for his dedication to his work. In fact, it was rumored that he was heir apparent to the superintendency when his superior retired two years from now.

"Very good. By the way, this is our poodle grooming class on your right." Davis paused, waiting for a reply.

"It seems to have quite an enrollment." Taylor reached into his pocket and removed a small notebook. "Let's see. You have approximately seven thousand people in your community. Is that correct?"

"Yes, that's quite true, give or take a little." Davis smiled, showing tobacco-stained teeth.

"What is the racial composition of your district, may I ask?"

"Offhand," said Davis slowly, "I'd say 68 percent white, 30 percent black, and 2 percent Spanish-speaking Americans."

Taylor meticulously entered these facts in his notebook.

"Say, this is our great books class. Quite a packer, I must say." Davis beamed proudly.

"Very interesting," Taylor said nonchalantly. He put his notebook in the side pocket of his suit coat. "Can you give me any background on your program's clientele?"

"Ah, you want to match interests with background." Davis smiled knowingly.

"Precisely," Taylor nodded.

"Well, we have the cream of the community here, I must admit. Wives of doctors, lawyers, businessmen, and a good many members from our civic organizations — Kiwanis, Lions, Rotary and the like, not to mention several of the husbands of the wives I referred to. They've all gone for community education in a big way."

"Do you have any blacks in the program?" Taylor said quietly, shuffling some change in his pocket.

"At the moment — No! We did have three in our high school equivalency group, but it closed out for lack of participants. It's really too bad." Davis frowned.

"Did you try circularizing the black community?" Taylor had his notebook in hand again.

"Yes, I did as a matter of fact. Unfortunately, I couldn't get much of a response. Evidently, they weren't interested." Davis toyed with his mustache, "I suppose it doesn't speak well of me."

"On the contrary," said Taylor, soothingly, "I'm sure you did the best you could."

Davis grinned happily. "Over there is our advanced Russian class. It's a big seller. I'm almost tempted to take it myself."

Taylor jotted down a few more items in his notebook. He was suddenly tired. He was only thirty-five, but he thought he was feeling twice his age tonight. The thought of the ride back grated against his nerves.

"I think I'm going to cut my visit short. I believe I've seen all I needed to." Taylor smiled weakly.

"Oh, I did want to show you our decoupage class; and our Beethoven class is a real gem." Davis whined in disappointment.

"I think you have a fine program. It's just too bad you don't have all of your community represented here." Taylor's face was nondescript.

"Well, I tried, as I said before. I tried hard. But they showed no interest." Davis spoke defensively. "What do you think of the community concept? Will you implement it?"

"I don't think so! Apparently we have too many low income people in the district." Taylor cleared his throat. "Based on your experiences, I would say that a community with 80 percent black and 20 percent white is not slated for much success in the project." Staring directly into the other man's eyes, Taylor said with a solemn gesture of finality, "I can only conclude that it's ideal for a middle class white community. Wouldn't you agree?"

Davis seemed to fall to pieces. "I don't know what to say."

Taylor shook his hand and headed for the door. The rain had slackened. In a happier tone, he turned back and shouted, "When you think of an answer, give me a call."

## QUESTIONS

1. How should Davis respond to Taylor?

2. Why were minority groups not participating?

3. Is it more advantageous in Middleberg's situation to have an all-white or an all-minority project? Discuss implications from both sides of the issue.

4. To what extent does Middleberg's project meet the criteria for community education?

5. Discuss what is meant by "circularizing the community."

6. Why does Taylor decide not to implement community education in his school district?

7. What might Davis do to involve the minority groups?

8. When investigating the implementation of community education, do most groups visualize community education as a rich person's or a poor person's program? Elaborate.

9. How successful would community education be in Taylor's community?

## ACTIVITIES

1. Role play a future meeting between Taylor and Davis.

2. Analyze the listing of courses offered:

   What section of the community had input?
   How might a greater variety of courses have been offered?

3. Prepare Taylor's presentation to his school board.

4. In small groups, discuss what could have been done in lieu of circularizing the community. Why did it work for one part of town and not the other?

5. Assume the superintendent called in Davis to ask about Taylor's visit. Role play their meeting.

CASE #6

## THE MAGNIFICENT PLAN

Art Matson, Farmingvale's aged but intensely active president of the board of education, strolled up to Superintendent Dale Roberts and tapped him on the shoulder. Grinning, he said, "Great work, Dale. Nine months ago, I wouldn't have believed it could be done. You surely picked a winner when you hired young Mackleroy." Matson's face was like cracking plaster, "Where is that young firebrand from Flint, Michigan?"

Roberts laughed loudly. "Mr. Community Education will be here on time. Don't you fret, Art."

"That young fellow certainly eliminated a lot of redundant efforts in the community. At least we're all on target now." Matson scratched his head. "I can't imagine how we ever got along without a coordinating board before."

Roberts nodded, in assent. Another board member entered the cafeteria. Having waved at him, he said, "The really good thing about it all is that it hasn't cost us a dime. We've got all seven buildings lighted up, more adults coming to school than I ever saw downtown on any one Saturday night, and a list of programs that looks like a college catalog."

"Excuse me, Dale. I think we're about ready to begin." Matson moved toward the center of a long metal lunch table to take his customary position. Everybody was in a happy mood. Community education was felt to be a raging success in Farmingvale and plaudits were freely exchanged among board members and between superintendent and board. At least half the members had actually participated in the community survey. They had called the effort a significant grassroots movement. As a result of their activity, they were closer than ever before to the heart of the community, or so they had surmised.

The board meeting was almost over when James Mackleroy dashed breathlessly into the building. In his hand was a sheaf of papers. Having quietly taken his seat on the left of the superintendent, he waited to be recognized.

Art Matson was too exhilarated by the events of the evening to fall prey to his occasional spell of irritability. Superintendent Roberts, however, was mildly upset; and he made it a point to convey his uneasiness to the younger man as soon as he sat down.

"Sorry, sir," Mackleroy whispered. "I had to get my figures straight."

"What figures are you talking about?" Roberts winced. His whispers grew loud. "I thought we had the budget down pat earlier this afternoon. We reviewed it together."

"This is something else, sir." Mackleroy smiled sheepishly. "Plans for new programs!"

"What?" spluttered Roberts. There was a hush in the room. Art Matson's eyes zeroed in on the superintendent, glaring at him until the superintendent lowered his head to stare at the table.

Five minutes later, Art Matson called on Superintendent Roberts to make his report on the community education program. Roberts expressed his thanks to the board for its support, briefly commented on the success of the program, and then turned to his community education director for a status report.

Mackleroy, a young man of twenty-seven, tall, blond, and stocky, with a huge grin on his face, calmly dispatched the facts. In effect, he swiftly explained, the program had cost the board nothing; and the response he received was a considerable grunt of satisfaction from his avid listeners.

But victory was not yet in sight according to the recent recipient of a master's degree in community education. This was made abundantly clear to the board. In fact, stated Mackleroy, the program was just beginning. Beaming, he said, "It is my plan to initiate a program for the eighteen to twenty-four year old, to resolve our dropout problem. I also intend to launch a meals-on-wheels program for the preschooler. I want to start a program that will improve the health of our senior citizens by taking them to doctors and dentists. I would like to see retired people helping other retirees. I look forward to industrial tie-ins to make our programs more occupationally oriented. I want . . . "

Art Matson interrupted, "Son, I want a lot of things too, but the honest truth is I just can't afford them. In simple English the district just can't afford to sponsor those kinds of activities. We don't have the money. I'm all for helping the senior citizen. I'm one myself. But every time you help us, you raise our taxes. And that's not really helping anybody."

Superintendent Roberts was aghast. He wanted in the worst way to shut his director's mouth, which was still open and ready to continue speaking.

Still smiling, Mackleroy said quietly to the president of the board, "Sir, these additional services will cost you only a small fraction of what they are actually worth *to people!*"

Roberts was on the verge of responding, but decided against it. There was nothing to be gained from quarreling with his subordinate in public.

Spurred on by peer approval, the president of the board said quite bluntly, "Let's be satisfied with what we have. Even if money weren't the issue here, and in the final analysis it's probably not, the role of the school would be. Our charge is to meet the educational and recreational needs of our citizens, not to solve the community's social, welfare, and health problems. Other agencies are better able to do these things." Matson cleared his throat. "I suggest we get on with other business. I'd like to get us all out of here before midnight tonight."

As the meeting struck a happier note, Mackleroy jammed his papers in his briefcase in disgust. Having completed his report, he left the room heatedly. No one, however, paid much attention to his departure. The meeting bustled along noisily.

Alone in the corridor, outside the board room, Mackleroy muttered to himself. "I guess it's about time I found another job." Silently, he added, "Where they really understand what community education is all about."

## QUESTIONS

1. The superintendent stated the program hadn't cost a dime. How was this possible?

2. Why was young Mackleroy in conflict with the board of education and the superintendent?

3. Why did Mackleroy attempt to add new projects to an already successful project?

4. Briefly explain whether or not Mackleroy's new programs were a responsiblity of community education.

5. How could the new plan be initiated with little or no cost?

6. How might Mackleroy have gotten involved in additional programs without stirring up the board?

7. Mackleroy was described as a trained community educator. Could an untrained coordinator have accomplished as much? Comment.

8. How is it possible to overcome the "let's go with what we have" attitude?

9. Mackleroy's philosophy of community education seemed to differ from that of the board. Who had the correct philosophy?

10. In Mackleroy's announcement of new programs, he did not discuss a closer tie of K-12 and community education. When should this idea be introduced? Enumerate advantages and disadvantages.

## ACTIVITIES

1. Prepare Mackleroy's response to the board.

2. In small groups, create a sample budget that might have been employed by Mackleroy.

3. Role play Mackleroy's defense of a need for additional programs.

4. Prepare a timetable depicting the nine-month process utilized by Mackleroy.

5. Farmingvale had a coordinating board. In small groups, discuss the role and purpose of such a board. Compare and discuss your answers.

6. Make a presentation to the class illustrating how Mackleroy could have prepared the board to accept an expanded program.

7. Discuss the pros and cons of the "it didn't cost us a dime" theory. Is this a way to sell community education, or should the board realize at the outset that community education does cost money?

8. In small groups, pick a new program (dropouts, preschool, senior citizen) and brainstorm how Mackleroy would initiate such a program.

## ANNOTATED READINGS

Berridge, Robert I. *The Community Education Handbook*, Midland, Michigan: Pendell Publishing Company, 1973. Chapter II, Initiating the Process; Chapter III, Site Selection. The sequential steps for initiating community education are discussed in Chapter II. The important phase of planning and the selection of schools, or other sites, constitute the primary focus of Chapter III.

Burden, Larry, and Whitt, Robert L. *The Community School Principal*, Midland, Michigan: Pendell Publishing Company, 1973, (pp. 175-196). Whitt discusses the role of the principal as he initiates community education in his attendance area. Illustrations and models emphasizing total involvement are highlighted in this section.

Carrillo, Tony S., and Heaton, Israel C. "Strategies for Establishing a Community Education Program," *Phi Delta Kappan*, Volume LIV, No. 3, November 1972, (pp. 165-167). The authors outline the steps taken by several Community Education Regional Centers to initiate community education projects. Experience has shown that in many communities wishing to implement a project there is a widespread zeal that develops, which often leads to a disjointed community effort. The authors contend that there must be a test of readiness on the part of key officials and the planning group prior to the initiation of the project. Steps are listed to accomplish this purpose.

Hickey, Howard W., and Van Voorhees, Curtis. *The Role of the School in Community Education*, Midland, Michigan: Pendell Publishing Company, 1969. Chapter VI, Community Education: A Developmental Process, written by Curtis Van Voorhees. The chapter contrasts the process with the program approach to community education. Presented in detail are the three phases which comprise community education: study, planning, and action.

Irwin, Martha, and Russell, Wilma. *The Community Is the Classroom*, Midland, Michigan: Pendell Publishing Company, 1971. Chapter II, Characteristics of a Community-Centered Curriculum. The overall impact of community education on the total K-12 curriculum is made apparent. Since the community is a laboratory for learning, this chapter outlines the potential of the lab that is in the school environment. The authors develop the idea that the school serves mainly as a coordinating center of a variety of experiences. In the planning of every community education project, it is suggested that grades K-12 be involved.

Kerensky, V. M., and Melby, Ernest O. *Education II — The Social Imperative*, Midland, Michigan: Pendell Publishing Company, 1971, (pp. 157-178). The authors provide a rationale for dealing with the twelve components of the modern community school. Background information is provided to strengthen the overall planning and implementing of community education. Particular attention is given to the establishment of goals and objectives.

Minzey, Jack, and LeTarte, Clyde E. *From Program to Process*, Midland, Michigan: Pendell Publishing Company, 1972, (pp. 45-77). Strong emphasis is placed on the commitment of the school administrative staff before implementation is initiated. School officials are cautioned to be aware of costs, financing, staffing, and, particularly, the new role which the school is assuming in its community.

Seay, Maurice F., and Associates. *Community Education: A Developing Concept,* Midland Michigan: Pendell Publishing Company, 1974, (pp. 147-168). This section of Seay's book sheds light on the composition and responsibility of administrative teams and decision-making bodies that plan and implement the community education concept. Several organizational flow charts for various-sized communities are illustrated and discussed. The practical aspects of implementation are contained in this section.

Totten, Fred. *The Power of Community Education,* Midland, Michigan: Pendell Publishing Company, 1970, (pp. 3-26). Graphic illustrations and multiple listings of responsibilities of school and community are focused upon in this section where a plea is made for interdisciplinary cooperation and planning in community education programs.

Whitt, Robert L. *A Handbook for the Community School Director,* Midland, Michigan: Pendell Publishing Company, 1971, (pp. 44-46). Although the setting for community education is in the community, much of what happens typically occurs within the school. The author discusses the program setting in the senior high school and in the elementary school.

# CHAPTER 3 Staffing the Project

The staffing needs for a community education project are much more complicated than that of most other endeavors. The problem lies with the complexity of the philosophy itself — a philosophy which covers a variety of existing personnel resources in the community. Thus, the project director, or community education coordinator, is working with the extremes of the personnel continuum — from the under-educated lay person to the college president.

To simplify the range, two basic categories must be examined. These are the professional and lay persons. Included in the professional category are the trained personnel of schools, city government, agencies, organizations and institutions. In the lay category are all non-professionals.

Within each category the coordinator deals with unusual circumstances. In some situations, he or she works with lay persons who are in leadership roles. In others, the coordinator works with professional persons who, because they are acting outside their usual professional roles, are classified as lay persons.

Working with various professionals, the coordinator must assume both a leadership and a cooperative role. As the resources of agencies, government and institutions come together in cooperative effort, the coordinator must work as a co-leader. And within the school system itself, the coordinator's role with staff, teachers, principals, and superintendent is mainly of leadership, but on a cooperative basis. There will be instances where the coordinator will work with teachers or agency personnel who are professional in their own field, yet who will be teaching hobby-type classes. This sometimes sets the scene for a different administrative situation.

In the role of community education coordinator, there is much contact with and use of lay persons. The lay person may assume the position of an administrator in community education, but, more often, he will be involved as a teacher within the program. Lay persons may be employes or volunteers. Again, varied problems may occur. When the lay person is paid as a staff member, a little more control is available to the coordinator. On the other hand, when the lay person is a volunteer, control is largely absent. An intensified inservice training program is usually required to familiarize lay persons with community education and the learning processes of adults.

The coordinator may also become involved in situations where professional teachers of children cannot teach adults or cannot adjust methods to noncredit courses. The coordinator may encounter the do-gooder who can't teach or the lay person who has an ax to grind.

The role of the coordinator in staffing is, indeed, complex, for it includes selection, training, administering, and evaluating. The coordinator must always look at his/her role as one of providing growth-facilitating opportunities to those persons, professional and lay, who become involved in community education. Although there are some inherent problems, coordinators generally find staffing to be a rewarding task.

The three cases chosen in this chapter depict situations which occur in the area of staffing. Over the years, the authors have faced in many different communities the particular problems explored in these cases.

In the first case the feasibility of lay coordination is breached. More and more communities around the country are asking if a coordinator must be a school person. The student will have an opportunity to make this determination after reading and discussing the case.

In employing a coordinator, most school boards, or screening committees, are faced with the choice of hiring a trained or untrained director or of hiring a local person or an outsider. The resultant dilemma is explored in the second case.

Problems associated with teachers in community education programming become the primary focus in the third case. Although only a small number of problems actually occur which are teacher related, these seem to stick in the minds of coordinators. As the case is assessed, the student will not only reach a decision on this particular situation, but

will also explore alternatives which should assist in avoiding future conflicts.

CASE #7

## THE LAY COORDINATOR

Principal George Armsely sat frowning behind a large gray metal desk. From time to time he would twirl around in his swivel chair to stare out the window. When the phone buzzed, he yelled into it, "Marjorie, I don't want any calls." His face was livid with anger.

"It's Mr. Blackstone. He wants to see you. He has an appointment, *he says*," she said, putting an equivocal touch on the last two words.

"I don't care what he says. And you can tell him that." He hung up the phone.

Sidney Blackstone knocked twice and then opened the door. Principal Armsely sat upright, aghast at the incredible temerity of the other man.

"I'm not speaking to you until I've finished talking with the superintendent. No lay person is going to tell me my business about community education, or any other thing that pertains to schools. I've got twenty-seven years of experience behind me. You're lucky to have twenty-seven days." Armsely's hands shook while he spoke.

Quite calmly, Sidney Blackstone took a chair at the far end of the room and waited.

"When you cool off, I'd like to exchange problems with you." Blackstone lighted his pipe and relaxed. "Do you mind?"

Armsely stared intently at Blackstone, but said nothing. His anger was replaced by a patriarchal composure.

"I realize I'm upsetting your routine. That I'm not making points with your faculty. And that your janitor doesn't like me very much. But your superintendent hired me to do a job, and I'm going to do it to the best of my ability." Blackstone puffed at his pipe. It had gone out. He struck a match and relighted it.

"I wish I did have more training in education, at least enough to get certified. But I don't plan to return to college to learn what I already know. I know this community. I've canvassed the neighborhood, developed block plans, and set up an interested and active lay advisory committee. I've got a program in full swing and a teaching staff composed of dedicated parents and teachers. Your school is alive with all kinds of constructive community activity." Blackstone stammered;

caught up in the worthiness of his cause, he was becoming more emotional.

Armsely couldn't restrain himself. "You said you wanted to exchange problems. So far all I hear is your problem. The argument is one sided," he said contemptuously.

"The gist of the problem, yours and mine," said Blackstone quietly, "is that we seem to be getting in each other's way. You let me run my show, and I'll stay out of your hair. Fair enough!"

Fingering through his thinning hair, Armsely lost his temper again. "I do not approve of lay teachers. We have plenty of qualified professional people in this school, or district, to fill almost any post. Although I went against my better judgment, I did finally consent to interview each of your proposed lay candidates. But even here you took matters into your own hands and hired those whom *you* saw fit." Armsely spat out the last few words with unconcealed venom.

"Those people, whom, you say, I hired indiscriminately, have been working out quite well in the classroom, despite the intrusions of your janitor, who is always jangling the keys in their doorways." Blackstone sighed, almost in desperation. "It would help immensely if you gave me a set of keys. Believe me, I value the school as much as you. I'd lock it up."

"The janitor is following my orders," interrupted Armsely. "When I want you to have keys, you'll get keys. Another thing — I suggest you get a college degree before you try getting certified. It always helps." Armsely laughed coarsely.

"All I ask for is a little cooperation." Blackstone was blushing. The sting of Armsely's last remark had lacerated his pride. "Your secretarial staff hang up on my people, refuse to volunteer information, and won't do typing of any kind for me. I have to turn to lay people for such help. I never expected to be treated this way." Blackstone bowed his head.

Armsely stood up and towered over Blackstone. "You saw what the faculty thought of you, Mr. High-and-Mighty, at the so-called inservice workshop you abortively conducted. You had your signs early in the program. You just overlooked them."

Without looking up, Blackstone groaned. "Why, you treated me as an object of ridicule. I can still hear you saying, 'Mr. Blackstone doesn't know much about education, not being certified, but he may be able to tell you something about your children and their families.' Then you repeatedly interrupted me until the floor was all yours." Blackstone dropped his pipe, and the ashes scattered across the floor.

"Look," said Armsely, "you work from 12:00 p.m. to 3:00 p.m. in the community, then later in the evening at school. I work from 7:00 a.m. to 7:00 p.m., if I'm lucky. Education is no game. It's a serious business. It

takes years of training and commitment." Armsely was smiling triumphantly.

Blackstone mumbled. "How can you run a class when the equipment
you need for the evening must be checked out by 4:00 p.m. and returned
by 8:00 p.m. How can you . . . " His voice trailed off.

Armsely puffed up his chest and strutted back to his desk. The phone
buzzed. Both men looked at each other, startled. It was the call Armsely
was expecting, but the buzzing noise had caught him off guard. His hand
trembled as he picked up the phone. He listened carefully to the voice
on the other end. It was the superintendent talking.

"Yes, sir. Thank you, sir. Thank you very much." He cradled the
phone and turned to Blackstone. "Let me be the first to inform you. The
teachers' new contract just negotiated community education out of the
district. You're out of a job."

Blackstone stared out the window through wet, glassy eyes. "Where
did I go wrong," he wondered.

## QUESTIONS

1. How was Blackstone upsetting the routine of the school?

2. Blackstone requested that the school program and community
   education each go its own way. Discuss the implications of such
   an arrangement.

3. Mr. Armsely with twenty-seven years experience in education
   did not approve of lay teachers. What might his argument be?

4. Discuss whether Armsely was correct in not giving Blackstone
   keys to the building.

5. How might Blackstone gain cooperation from the secretarial
   staff?

6. Can school-owned equipment be used in community education
   programs? Comment.

7. What kinds of problems may be expected to arise when a lay
   person is hired to coordinate a community education project?

8. Why did the superintendent employ a lay coordinator? What are
   the legal implications?

9. Why would the teacher's new contract negotiate community education out of the district?

10. How would you describe Armsely as an administrator?

## ACTIVITIES

1. Role play the superintendent hiring Blackstone.

2. Rewrite the case illustrating how a lay coordinator might have enhanced Mr. Armsely's project.

3. Prepare an inservice plan that would have prompted the professional teaching staff to accept Blackstone.

4. In small groups, discuss the content of college classes which Mr. Blackstone might have taken to assist him in performing his duties.

5. Compile a list of the problems as assessed by Blackstone and Armsely. Compare lists and, as a class exercise, discuss alternative solutions.

6. Rewrite the end of the case so that community education is maintained. Role play a meeting between the superintendent and Armsely to discuss problems.

7. Role play a meeting called by lay teachers and lay citizens to protest the ending of community education. What arguments might be involved?

8. As a class, discuss how the teachers could negotiate out community education if community education were really operating according to philosophy.

**CASE #8**

## THE DEADLOCK

The screening committee for the selection of a community education director for the Charlestown public school system had reached an impasse. Having narrowed down their choices to two candidates, the committee members were unable to make a decision.

The committee, comprised of two administrators, two teachers, and two parents, would at one moment opt for the local candidate, the next seem to favor the out-of-towner. Finally, two parents, George Daly and Louise Cross, joined forces with Irene Newman, an elementary school principal, and pushed hard for the young woman from Canterbury, Ohio.

The result was that Assistant Superintendent Robert Hemlein, Coach Arthur Rankin, and Betty Sweetwater, a home economics teacher, quickly revealed that they were strongly allied with the local candidate.

After another hour of haggling, Louise Cross calmly suggested that they once again review both the strong and weak points of each candidate; this time, however, using a slightly different strategy. It was her idea that a chalkboard listing might provide them with some additional insights. She volunteered to do the writing. Assistant Superintendent Hemlein, on the verge of leaving the conference room in disgust, stayed to listen to a football joke that Art Rankin was telling George Daly. All three laughed, and the antagonisms of the group vanished.

"O.K." grunted Hemlein, "I think I can sit patiently for another hour. It'll only prove that Art and Betty and I are right." He was smugly satisfied, having made an unchallenged statement.

Louise Cross was at the chalkboard. On one side of the board she wrote Larry Petersen; on the other, Deborah Stiles. Under each name she wrote strengths and weaknesses.

"I think we're ready," she said, smiling. She added, "At least I am."

Arthur Rankin was the first to speak. "Plus number one I'd say is that Larry is home-grown talent . . . Charlestown's native son!"

The chalk squeaked against the slate. "Who's next?" queried Louise.

"Larry's the perfect age," said Assistant Superintendent Hemlein. "He's young, vigorous, athletic, and an ex-football star, someone the folks really admire."

Louise Cross scratched on the slate the key ideas, adding twenty-seven, the age of Larry Petersen. She saw a raised hand. "Betty, what is it that you wish to add?"

Betty Sweetwater, a fourth-year teacher at the Griswold Junior High School, said softly, "I'd like to point out that Larry's father has been a respected businessman in this community for twenty-five years. I think he's helped just about everybody at one time or another."

"Thank you, Betty," said Louise Cross, writing as rapidly as she could. The chalk broke and fell to the floor. Picking it up, she said, "Any more comments? Some weaknesses, perhaps." She grinned.

Assistant Superintendent Hemlein cleared his throat. "It might be wise to note that Larry has a good deal of administrative potential. I've been seriously considering him for a junior high school principalship for over a year now." Coach Rankin wore an expression of shock on his face.

Louise Cross laughed. "However irrelevant to the topic, I must admit that Larry was the best newspaper boy I ever had." The group joined her in laughter.

George Daly tried to speak above the burst of laughter. "My son Ralph thinks Larry is the best teacher he ever had. It's obvious that he works well with people." Daly, Vice-president of Trust of the Charlestown National Bank, felt himself suddenly favoring the Petersen boy again.

"Ah, but what about his weaknesses," chimed in Louise Cross. "Or can we find none?"

Art Rankin was quick to concede that Larry had no experience in community education. Nevertheless, he added that Larry did know the community better than any outsider.

"I believe," said Rankin, "that Larry is devoted to the concept. He's a born community education man. He revealed as much during his interview."

Having remained silent since Louise Cross began grating her chalk against the chalkboard, Irene Newman now spoke up. She snapped, "Art Rankin, you know about as much as I do about community education — nothing." Shaking her head, she said, "How can you possibly say with any conviction that Larry is a born community education man? We're only beginning to learn what community education is all about."

Rankin blushed, then turned sullen. He regretted he hadn't studied the subject more than perfunctorily in preparing to serve on the screening committee.

Pausing only momentarily to let her remarks seep into the group's thinking, Irene Newman said, "Larry is a fine boy, comes from one of Charlestown's best families, and no doubt will make an admirable principal one day, but he is not a specialist in community education. And we need a specialist if we're going to get the program off the ground." She stopped to catch her breath.

"I agree with Irene," said Louise Cross, waving her chalk. "The young lady we interviewed last week may not know much about our community, but she does know about community education."

"It's true," said Assistant Superintendent Hemlein, scratching his head, "that Miss Stiles has a fine track record. She was extremely successful as a community education director in a town approximately our size for two years. But how will our folks treat her when they know she was chosen over their native son? Larry has quite a following." Hemlein shifted his position to relieve some of his discomfort. He was tired of sitting and yearned to exercise his long wiry legs.

"We might have added," beamed Betty Sweetwater, "that Miss Stiles has a master's degree in community education with a minor specialization in administration. Right now Larry has only fifteen credits earned toward his master's degree."

Assistant Superintendent Hemlein inserted, "All in administration, which you neglected to mention." He glared at Miss Sweetwater until she squirmed in her seat.

"Give her a year!" said George Daly. "She's young, about the same age as Larry. And single! She can pick up her things and leave anytime without having her life disrupted." Yawning, Daly moved over to the coffee urn. Finding it empty, he returned to his seat irritated.

"I was very impressed with her during her interview," said Louise Cross. "She is both intelligent and amiable, not to mention polished."

"She seems to have all the answers," said Assistant Superintendent Hemlein sardonically. "That's for sure!"

"That depends on who's asking the questions," giggled Art Rankin. The group forced a feeble laugh.

"I agree, Art," said Louise Cross. "We don't know much about community education. That's why we need a specialist. We can't afford to flounder around." Louise picked up her pad and tore three sheets from it, folded each sheet and tore them again. With six slips of paper in her hand, she said, "I suggest we take a secret ballot. I'm willing to abide by the decision of the majority."

"I think that's a splendid idea," said Assistant Superintendent Hemlein, anxious to eat dinner. The clock was rapidly approaching 8:00 p.m.

"All in favor say aye," said Irene Newman, equally anxious to wind up the meeting.

The group was overwhelmingly unanimous in its outcry.

The slips of paper were passed out by Louise Cross, who also picked them up seconds later. At the table next to the chalkboard she counted the votes.

Facing the group with the results, Louise Cross said, "Our community education director is _____ !"

## QUESTIONS

1. What was the makeup of the screening committee? How good was its representation? Who else might have been included on it?

2. Whom would you have chosen? Why?

3. Larry Petersen was described as being the perfect age for the job. Is there a perfect age?

4. Larry is "devoted to the concept." Is this a strong statement for his case?

5. What kind of arguments can be made for selecting the nonexperienced local director and the experienced out-of-towner?

6. Since Miss Stiles has proven herself with a successful two-year project, is not a specialist needed to initiate a community education project? Comment.

7. If Petersen gets the job, what training should he receive and where should he get it? How could he take time for training when he is on the job full-time?

8. Does the committee give any indication that its choice will be influenced by the fact that one of the candidates is a male and the other a female?

9. What conditions in Charlestown might influence the decision toward a trained director vs. an untrained one? Toward a male or female?

## ACTIVITIES

1. List, as Louise Cross did, the attributes of each on the chalkboard. Analyze and discuss.

2. From reference material, document the case of the local director

vs. the outside director.

3. List on the board the steps to the initiation of community education. Contrast both directors in the light of each step.

4. Role play Miss Stiles' appearance before the board.

5. Role play Mr. Petersen's appearance before the board.

6. Poll the class to determine the choice of directors.

7. Rewrite the case with Miss Stiles as director.

8. Rewrite the case with Mr. Petersen as director.

9. Interview three experienced community education coordinators. How would they react to the case?

**CASE #9**

## THE DROPOUT INTERVIEWS

Community education was booming in the city of Bartonberry, and Hal August, the project director, was exceptionally pleased. Eighteen courses had been successfully run in the spring with above average participation, and chances were that the forthcoming fall would be even better. Three courses, on the other hand, had experienced significant attendance problems. Each had begun boasting an enrollment of approximately twenty adults, but had concluded with no more than a dismal handful. In an effort to improve the program, August had decided to interview a few of the dropouts from the failing courses. More important, however, was the fact that August was confronted with the grim necessity of eliminating any teachers who might in any way be considered detrimental to the program's continued success. It was not a simple task, for all three of the unsuccessful teachers wanted to be rehired in the fall.

Contributing to his problem was that all three teachers were thought to be excellent teachers within the system. Doug Barnes, for example, was a crackerjack history teacher. Barnes-taught students bragged about knowing more history than any other students in the school. Barnes was also a basketball coach who was consistently victorious. He related well with students; by and large, they idolized him.

Ann Tomilson was equally a fine teacher, according to her peers. She was active in every organization in the district. She paraded around the city, fighting for every cause that might even remotely be identified with the so-called plight of the downtrodden. She was the leader in the program to offer breakfast to preschoolers from impoverished families. The mothers loved her, and the superintendent was seriously considering her for a central office position in the area of federal programs. At thirty, Miss Tomilson's great love was the community in which she laboriously worked. Her pace was astounding. Indeed, many wondered how she could be such an excellent teacher and still be so active in the field. They envied her dedication.

Robert Bannerly was extraordinarily different from the other two project teachers. Nobody liked him, but everyone feared him. He was the most militant person in the school. As president of the Bartonberry

Teachers' Association, he had negotiated, this year, a contract that both the administration and the board would long remember. Next year, they were anticipating much worse.

Rumor had it that the superintendent had offered Bannerly a principalship in one of the district's two junior high schools. Rumor also had it that Bannerly had, without hesitation, turned down the offer. No one was quite sure what had happened, but all believed that Bannerly was dedicated to the teachers who supported him.

In view of the reputations of all three project teachers, August was hoping that the interviews with the dropouts would reveal no more than a chance relationship between declining enrollments and teaching styles. If he dismissed any one of three, his program might be severely hurt. If he dismissed all three, he, himself, might be in trouble. In any case, he had to find out the facts. After he had them, his professional ethics would guide him to his decision.

Ernest Jones, twenty-one years old, a black high school dropout, was his first interviewee. Jones sat across from August, twiddling his thumbs nervously. It was nine o'clock in the morning.

"Ernest, I am very pleased you were able to come today. I consider it a personal favor." August sighed, wondering how to begin. He didn't like the role of interrogator.

"No problem, Mr. August. I'm on the second shift now. Don't begin work until three."

August looked relieved. "Is that why you stopped coming to your high school equivalency class?"

"Yeh, I guess so." Jones stared at the Band-Aid on his thumb. "Yeh, I guess that's how it was."

"Did they transfer you to the second shift halfway through the term?" probed August.

"Yes," answered Jones, uneasily.

"I thought you were big on getting your high school diploma." August leaned over to bridge the small gap that separated the two men. "Was that all a story?" Suddenly changing his point of inquiry, August asked, "Did you put in for the transfer to the second shift?" August waited for what seemed to be forever for the younger man's reply.

Jones suddenly laughed, "Man, that was no class. That was a soul story. I didn't learn anything. I suppose I heard about a lot of good things happening in the community, but I wasn't learning any English. That lady was way out. My mother thinks she's great, but I don't read that teacher noways. All she kept harping on was man's inhumanity to man. I don't mean to get her in trouble. She's a good lady. I just don't understand her. Dig?" Stretching his arms, Jones yawned. He seemed more uninhibited, having revealed himself.

"You mean she's disorganized and doesn't stick to the topic."

"That's it, man. All the way." Jones smiled.

"Would you return if I changed teachers?" August was unsure of the reply he wanted to hear.

"No, it's too late for that. I'll be on the second shift for the next six months," Jones responded somewhat apologetically.

"Maybe, next spring?" August shook the hand of the young factory worker warmly.

"Maybe." Jones liked the firm handshake of the man who was probably no older than his brother Fred, his senior by ten years. The handshake conveyed a friendly feeling to him. Perhaps he would be back.

"Thanks very much," said August as he walked Jones to his car. "I really appreciate your visit."

August interviewed five other people during the next three hours, skipping his lunch to get the job done. The results were the same. All of the dropouts confirmed what Jones had said. Miss Tomilson was a do-gooder, but not a teacher. The dropouts had needed simply ordinary facts presented in a coherent manner, and they had received instead the gushings of a zealot.

In the afternoon Pauline Clements, another project dropout, responded to his request for course evaluations. Mrs. Clements, the mother of five children, most of whom were married, had been at forty-five searching for an interesting diversion to help occupy her time. Though she had never finished high school, she had always been an avid reader of history. School, she had thought, would bring her closer together with people who shared her interests. Although she was still deeply in love with her husband, she had never come to appreciate either his job as fireman or his overwhelming enthusiasm for spectator sports. While he talked sports or firefighting to anyone in the neighborhood who would listen, she read her book-of-the-month historical selection. Now that her children needed her less and less, she turned almost completely to the past for her salvation.

Mrs. Clements did not mince words about why she had dropped the course. She was, in fact, almost irate as she relived the situation.

"I came to Mr. Barnes' class to learn about history, to discuss great achievements, heroic deeds, to rediscover our cultural heritage, to explore world history, and to share my ideas with others. But what did I get — formal assignments, study guide questions, and a lot of memorizing and tests. In addition, I was treated as a child. You should have heard him say 'class sit up and pay attention.' Why I was never so humiliated in all my life." Mrs. Clements' face was flushed.

The interview was short and to the point. August thanked the middle-aged housewife for her frank portrayal of the facts and for her visit to the school. He also apologized for any embarrassment she had experienced during the course. Most of the comments made by subsequent interviewees zeroed in on the same problem.

George Appleby, a local plumber of some fifty years, complained about being treated like a teenager and about the number of tests he had been required to take. Mildred Portley, a senior citizen of long standing in the community, admitted that the course had been taking up too much of her time. "It wasn't fun," she remarked, "it was hard work. The young man was dead serious about making us memorize the history of Western civilization. I simply didn't have the time for all those tests."

Gregory Pace, a professed history buff, on the other hand, said that he had enjoyed the course very much. Moreover, he made it quite evident that his dropping out had been attributable to a personal problem, not a scholastic one. Anna Lorne carefully explained that she had nothing against the professor or the school. She just had to learn all over again why she was a high school dropout in the first place. "School," she said, "has always been a drag for me. I don't like it now, and I never will. I thought maybe if I went back — after all, it's been ten years since I quit — I might get to like it. I was wrong," she said sadly. Linda Freedman, on being interviewed, quickly exclaimed, "It was an awful course. All busy work. I shiver every time I think of it."

It was late afternoon before the third set of interviews began. Douglas Wallace, a heavy-set, gray-haired man of about fifty-five was first to arrive. He was one of Bartonberry's independent grocers, a butcher by trade.

August's hand was lost in the meaty palm of the butcher's when the two men shook hands. "I'm happy to see you again, Mr. Wallace. It's always a pleasure." August flashed on a neon smile. Then his jowls seemed to collapse. He looked exhausted. There were circles under his eyes.

"Why don't you drop in the store sometime? I'd like to have you meet the Mrs." Wallace sat down. His weight made the chair creak.

"I will," August's voice trailed off, "one of these days." Catching hold of himself, he quickly added, "I think you know why you're here. I tried to make that abundantly clear on the telephone when I asked for your help. We want to improve our program. We want everyone to feel that it is meeting his or her needs. The only way we can determine this is through feedback. We need your opinions. This is especially true because you were a dropout. Somehow we may have failed you." August took a deep breath. "May I ask why you felt inclined to drop out of the program?"

The butcher scowled in his recollections. "Mr. August, I came to learn about photography, and all I heard from Mr. Bannerly was teacher militancy, unions, contractual agreements, and a return to the three R's to reform the schools. The administration was criticized; and the board was denounced, but nothing — nothing — did I hear about photography that I didn't already know; and believe me, I know next to nothing. I got a thirty-five millimeter camera from my oldest boy for Christmas that I still don't know how to operate." Wallace wiped his perspiring forehead with an oversized handkerchief.

When the meeting concluded, Wallace promised he would give the program a second chance; for it was his sincere desire to understand more about photography. The prospects of such a hobby had always fascinated him, but only lately with his sons full grown and helping out in the business was he getting a little free time to cultivate his interests.

August interviewed five other dropouts, and the statements given checked with one exception. The last one was given by a young man of twenty-two who seemed to have gotten all he needed out of the course in the first few weeks. Since his withdrawal, he had taken a job at a camera shop and was making substantial headway in his newly chosen field. The young man's comments about Bannerly had made August have certain reservations about dismissing the instructor. The accolades paid Bannerly by the young man were certainly noteworthy. The problem was to sift the right answer from the facts he had received today, if, indeed, there was a right answer. Perhaps, there was only a best answer.

The setting sun could be seen from his window as he pondered the decisions he must make for the good of the project and for the sake of the community. If he refused to hire any one of the three, there would undoubtedly be some reverberations, but if he rejected all three, then what? The same thoughts kept recurring to him, thoughts that he had grappled with all day, but what action he should take was still to be determined.

## QUESTIONS

1. What would happen if August fired one or two of the teachers? If he fired all three?

2. What is the argument for maintaining all three teachers?

3. What would your decision be regarding the teachers? How do you justify your answer?

4. Explain whether the arguments of the participants were justified?

5. Should noncredit courses be taught differently than credit courses? Comment.

6. What type of inservice might August have conducted for his teachers?

7. How should a community education coordinator screen teachers?

8. What are advantages and disadvantages of using volunteer teachers in community education projects?

9. In a situation where some teachers are paid and some are volunteers, what problems might arise?

10. Why would August's problem have been different if the three teachers in question had been lay persons?

## ACTIVITIES

1. In groups, discuss August's method of following up on dropouts. What other methods might be employed?

2. Role play a meeting between August and Barnes to discuss the class.

3. Role play a meeting between August and Tomilson to discuss the class.

4. Role play a meeting between August and Bannerly to discuss the class.

5. Extend the case into next semester:

   Write what might happen if all three are re-employed.
   Write what might happen if all are dismissed.
   Write what might happen if certain individuals are dismissed.

6. In small groups, discuss how August might change the teaching style of each.

7. Role play August's discussion with the superintendent regarding his decision.

8. In groups, list the advantages and disadvantages of using lay teachers and professional teachers.

## ANNOTATED READINGS

Berridge, Robert I. *The Community Education Handbook*, Midland, Michigan: Pendell Publishing Company, 1973. Chapter V, The Role of the Coordinator. The chapter emphasizes the need for a full-time coordinator to implement a community education project. The coordinator is described as the key to project development. The argument against employing a part-time coordinator is that he/she is often only a supervisor and thus does not have time to work in the community. In the chapter the various roles of the coordinator are described in large and small communities and in elementary, junior high, and senior high schools. The role expectations of the coordinator are also described.

Burden, Larry, and Whitt, Robert L. *The Community School Principal*, Midland, Michigan: Pendell Publishing Company, 1973, (pp. 95-121). This chapter deals with building a coordinated staff for day and evening involvement of professional staff members. Areas such as selection, inservice, and evaluation are examined from the community school principal's point of view. Also addressed is the effect of total professional day school staff involvement on the community education program.

Hickey, Howard W., and Van Voorhees, Curtis. *The Role of the School in Community Education*, Midland, Michigan: Pendell Publishing Company, 1969. Chapter VII, Community Schools: Staffing and Training, written by Gerard E. Keidel, Jr. The selection and training of community education coordinators are discussed in the chapter. The author also emphasizes the need for training in other positions. Included are sections on the training of the principal, teachers, superintendents, and auxiliary personnel.

Janove, Ethan B. "The Man in the Middle," *Community Education Journal*, Volume I, No. 1, February 1971, (pp. 14-16). The author points out that the director must, with purpose and direction and a knowledge of his audience, inspire interest, involvement, and innovation.

Kerensky, V. M., and Melby, Ernest O. *Education II — The Social Imperative*, Midland, Michigan: Pendell Publishing Company, 1971, (pp. 152-154). The emphasis here is on building a strong rationale for effective leadership in educational programs. Ten suggestions which encourage enthusiastic leadership are offered to administrators.

Minzey, Jack, and LeTarte, Clyde E. *From Program to Process*, Midland, Michigan: Pendell Publishing Company, 1972, (pp. 161-192). This section of the text examines the types of staffing used in community education programming from volunteer to professional personnel. Some consideration is given to the human, technical, and conceptual skills required of staff members involved in community education.

Nance, Everette E. "The Community Education Coordinator," *Community Education Journal*, Volume II, No. 5, November 1972, (pp. 52-55). The coordinator is described as the key to success in a community education project. The selection process of the coordinator is discussed. Included are important character traits to the position. The role of the coordinator is viewed as teacher, counselor, organizer, administrator, supervisor, communicator, and human relations builder.

Seay, Maurice F., and Associates. *Community Education: A Developing Concept,* Midland, Michigan: Pendell Publishing Company, 1974, (pp. 119-144). This chapter deals with the comprehensive training needed for the key leadership roles required for successful community education programs. Special attention is given to training, learning, and field experience needed by a community education administrator. Human, technical, and conceptual skills are highlighted in the chapter.

Totten, Fred. *The Power of Community Education,* Midland, Michigan: Pendell Publishing Company, 1970, (pp. 128-158). Totten illustrates how community members may be involved in leadership roles in community education and discusses the effects such involvement will have on their personal lives.

Whitt, Robert L. *A Handbook for the Community School Director,* Midland Michigan: Pendell Publishing Company, 1971, (pp. 41-44, 59-62). Chapter VI, The Community School Director and Community Interest Groups. Discussed are the qualities of a community school director and a summary of his duties. Also discussed is the relationship of the director to the principal and teaching staff. The author lists twenty-two power groups and their contact persons.

# CHAPTER 4 Coordinating Community Efforts

One of the major characteristics of a well-developed community education program is how well the existing organizations, service clubs, and social service agencies are being involved in the total program. Long before the concept and philosophy of community education came into existence, primary services to local community members were being accomplished through organizations and agencies. The city recreation department, along with the YMCA, boys clubs and 4-H, to name a few, were doing a good job providing recreational activities in most communities. Service clubs, such as the Jaycees, Optimists, and Lions, were picking up some additional special, seasonal activities in the local communities. Social services were being provided by a larger number of health and welfare agencies common to most communities across the country.

Looking objectively at the public schools as a delivery system for services, one would be hard pressed to find another agency or organization that has such a good communication system with the grassroot levels of the community. When a school system enters into the cooperative philosophy of sharing resources, new life is generated into the community, and a powerful vehicle for change and service comes into existence.

When and how this cooperative effort takes place is the basis for the case studies in this chapter. The authors feel that organization and agency involvement should grow from the very conception of the community education philosophy. To exclude these groups from initial program development is to violate a primary principle of community education.

Community education specialists must be aware that any new attempt by an outside organization to begin working cooperatively with a particular established organization will, perhaps, engender a modicum of mistrust. Through a carefully developed plan of action, whereby the school does, indeed, enhance the serviceability of a specific organization, barriers will soon turn into pathways of joint cooperation. From the authors' point of view, the school must be the initiator of such action. Because organizations have operated in a vacuum for many years, it is difficult for them to take an aggressive role.

With these thoughts in mind the student is encouraged to read the following cases, all of which are aimed at building a coordinated effort in the community.

The first case deals with a community school coordinator who has built a strong community school program, but has left out organizations, agencies, and city government in developing a total community education project. Because of a policy change advocated by a new superintendent with previous community education experience, the coordinator must now try to incorporate these neglected agencies and organizations into her total community education program. The second case, which concerns two different approaches to community education, highlights the process vs. program aspect of community involvement. The final case, dealing with community council involvement in community education, illustrates what not to do when trying to gain community involvement through the community council approach.

**CASE #10**

## THE COMMUNITY WAY

Eleanor Mays waited enthusiastically for her turn to meet with the new superintendent of the Maitland City School District. She had arrived thirty minutes early to make sure she would be on time for her appointment.

All week the superintendent had been conferring with the directors of various subject matter areas. While she waited for James Hollihan, the director of English, to conclude his progress report, she filled several pages of a pad with ideas she wished to share with the superintendent. She was exceedingly proud of her record as the director of the district's community education project and looked forward to the praise she thought due her.

Almost singlehandedly she had built the program from a handful of courses and about sixty people in one school into more than a dozen courses in three different buildings, one secondary school and two elementary schools. Presently there were approximately four hundred participants in the program.

The board of education was strongly in favor of community education and extremely pleased with Miss Mays' work. So high was community support that there hadn't been a bond levy defeat since the project's first anniversary. Now, three years later, the members of the board looked largely to community education for the continued support of the entire school system.

When Gil Davis, the harbinger of community education, resigned as superintendent to retire on a small ranch in Arizona, the board became frantic in its search for a replacement. The chief administrator who would replace Davis, the members unanimously agreed, had to be an experienced community educator.

Craig Donaldson, the board's choice after a long search, stood in the doorway of his office smiling. The director of English pumped his hand happily. "You can count on me, Dr. Donaldson," gushed the graying Hollihan as he moved into the outer office.

"I know I can," purred Donaldson, a man in his middle forties who both looked and dressed surprisingly youthful. "Miss Mays, it's a pleasure to see you again," he added, turning toward the community education director. "Come in, please."

Eleanor Mays bounced up from her chair, drawn by the warmth in the chief administrator's voice. When she was seated again in Donaldson's office, he gently closed the door.

"Do you mind if I smoke?" asked Donaldson suavely.

"No-no!" Miss Mays beamed. "I just love pipes."

"Would you care for a cup of coffee?" Donaldson lighted his pipe without taking his eyes off the community education director, seated directly across from him. Miss Mays shook her head. "Tea, perhaps? I do believe we have a few teabags around." Again, her head moved from side to side.

"Tell me, Miss Mays, how is your project progressing, and what future plans do you have for it?" The superintendent settled back in his chair comfortably.

Miss Mays eagerly moved forward in her chair. "The project continues to expand," she said effervescently while her blue eyes sparkled. "I'm happy to report that I'll be starting a new program in another elementary school this fall."

Donaldson listened intently to the attractive young devotee of community education. He was impressed by her verve and her commitment to the project. Formerly a home economics teacher, she had, in her fourth year with the district, zealously assumed the directorship, despite her lack of formal training in the field. Watching her exuberant gestures, he was reminded of his own exciting experiences in community education.

"Here is a list of my present course offerings. As you can see, it is quite extensive." She grinned. "And participation is excellent."

"Fine," said Donaldson, examining the list. "It's obvious the program is self-supporting," he said as an afterthought.

Miss Mays laughed with a certain sense of abandonment. "You should see our profits!"

"How many agencies are involved with you in the project?" asked Donaldson casually.

"Why, none!" Miss Mays was somewhat abashed. As if in defense, she quickly blurted out, "Mr. Davis, our former superintendent, made it quite clear to me that it was the school district's project and that agency and organizational involvement would only mean interference in the long run. He used to say, 'Miss Mays, we've got a good thing going here. Let's keep it that way!' "

"Do you agree?" Superintendent Donaldson toyed with his pen.

"I never gave the situation much thought. I merely followed orders," said Miss Mays cautiously, her embarrassment turning into annoyance.

"I suggest you give the subject plenty of thought during the next few days." Donaldson folded his arms. "What you've been alluding to is a community school. It is my intention to promote community education. The community school is only a delivery system for a much broader concept of community education."

"I really don't have enough time for that kind of involvement." Miss Mays stiffened. Her cheeks were flushed and her forehead wrinkled. "But I'll do my best."

"You'll have the time. It's a lot easier than you think once you get started. Furthermore, if you need assistance, indicate, in the plan I expect you to shortly submit, precisely what kind of and how much."

Miss Mays squirmed in her chair, "Plan?" She shuffled her notes nervously.

"We're going to organize a community team, first on paper, and later in the field. I want you to begin cooperating with clubs, organizations, agencies, institutions, and industrial concerns as soon as possible."

"Yes, sir." Miss Mays' eyes widened. She was fearful of the task that lay before her. Yet the possibilities began to challenge and excite her imagination. Suddenly, she saw her role as community education director in a new and impressive light.

The superintendent walked toward the door as Miss Mays rose from her chair. "You've been doing a splendid job, Eleanor. You've produced wonders in the system. Let's see you in action in the community."

Miss Mays brightened. "Thank you." She looked directly in the superintendent's eyes. "I won't disappoint you."

"I want to see you back here next Tuesday with the plan that's going to lead us to community education." Donaldson smiled. "We've got a considerable amount of work ahead of us. Of that you can be sure. But we'll do it. Together," he added, shaking her small hand.

Miss Mays left the superintendent's office feeling dazed. Tuesday was just four days away. It was going to be a hectic weekend. But she was anxious to get started.

## QUESTIONS

1. What early indication in the case suggested that Miss Mays might eventually have confronted a problem in the community despite what actually occurred later in the case?

2. Cite several statements in the case that indicated there was a lack of process in Miss Mays' project.

3.  What basic philosophy of community education is violated in Miss Mays' statement on profits? Provide a rationale for your answer.

4.  Define community school and community education as Superintendent Donaldson might define them.

5.  Discuss how the agencies in Maitland City might feel about community education. Explain whether these feelings would be justified.

6.  Expand upon how the role of community education might take on a " . . . new and impressive light" for Miss Mays in Maitland City.

7.  In another situation where involvement of community agencies and organizations was evident, what percentage of programs and involvement might evolve in a typical community of 25 thousand population? Outline briefly what the program might look like.

8.  Suggest what Miss Mays might do first in developing her plan for expanding community education in Maitland to include community agencies. Comment on whether her task is going to be easy or difficult.

9.  What is the superintendent's role in assisting Miss Mays in completing her task?

## ACTIVITIES

1.  In small groups, develop a timetable and plan for involving agencies and organizations in Miss Mays' community education project.

2.  Role play a meeting between Miss Mays and ten predominant agencies in Maitland as she tries to involve these agencies in community education.

3.  List some strategies that would show how the new superintendent might offset negative reactions from organizations and agencies.

4.  Make a list of people in the district, in addition to the superintendent, who might assist Miss Mays in completing her task.

5. Brainstorm a list of as many agencies and organizations as you can that might become involved in a community education program. Cite the specific way in which each might participate.

CASE #11

## FREEDOM OF CHOICE

The morning session of the regional seminar for community education coordinators concluded on an inspirational note. Most coordinators reported large enrollments, a variety of course offerings, and excellent attendance records. Everyone was excited about the progress of the region; and all were convinced that community education was really catching on. On the same token, nobody had encountered any significant problems; nor were they expecting any. Continued success seemed to be the order of the day.

At lunch Bob Harvesty, the community education director for the Sunnytown School District, admitted somewhat reluctantly to his former community education classmate, Chuck Johnson, that his project was still in the information-gathering stage. Prior to his arrival at the seminar, he had been quite pleased with the progress he was making. Now, after listening to a couple of dozen success stories, Harvesty was a bit embarrassed about having accomplished so much less than his peers. What troubled him most was the apparent good fortune of Johnson, the young man seated directly across from him, who had a program in full swing with twenty-three classes on the books, all filled to capacity. Johnson had completed his training and accepted his first position the same time Harvesty had. A few months ago, both men had been novices in the field of community education; today Johnson was talking like an old pro. And he was collecting quite a following. People were inclined to listen to the towering blond youth who appeared to exude confidence with every gesture.

Pointing his fork at Harvesty's face, Johnson spluttered through a mouthful of green beans, "Bob, you were always too big on the process nonsense. The process is only a vehicle to arrive at a program. It is not an end in itself. If you can anticipate needs, you can virtually do away with process. Once you have attained program stature, process is without meaning." Johnson pinned a piece of beef against his plate with his fork and began hacking away at it with his knife. Watching the progress of his knife, he added, "Look, I know how enamored you are with process, but believe me, if process is characterized by involvement, programs epitomize involvement. Commitment is obvious if people enroll in your program and attend class week after week. It is nonexistent when you are collecting door-to-door responses from people who may offer answers, but rarely participation."

Harvesty, a small dark man in his middle thirties, sipped his coffee quietly. His deep blue eyes were pensive, and his forehead was wrinkled with concern. "Maybe, I'm wrong. Yet I just can't help thinking that classwork is not the mark of success in a community education project. I'd like to think that community education is people working together with classwork being only one of several possible outcomes from their consolidated efforts."

"Bob, whatever my community needs, they'll get. Rest assured." Johnson lighted a cigar and blew a torrent of smoke across the small dining table.

"You mean they'll get what you think they need, don't you?" Harvesty fanned the cloud of smoke away from his face. His eyes were beginning to tear.

Johnson dragged deeply on his cigar. Smoke poured out of his mouth as he talked. "What's the difference, Bob? Tell me, does anybody truly know what he wants? Wouldn't you agree that my way is much more expedient for getting things done!" He leaned back in his chair, glancing at some of the other tables. He was bored and made no effort to conceal it.

Harvesty forced a smile, feeling patronized. "You sound like some kind of despot — a master manipulator!"

"If you feel free, you are free." Johnson laughed. "My participants are free to choose from a variety of selections, and they enjoy doing it. I merely attempt to make a number of options available, in keeping with their implied or expressed needs. What more could I do?"

"You're serious!" Harvesty was indignant.

"All kidding aside, Bob, I think I'll continue to reach more of my community through our classroom associations than you will parading around the community with your steering committee looking for a direction to steer in." Johnson looked at his watch. "It's time for the next session."

"Chuck, I'm willing to wager that before long I'll have a half dozen programs going compared to your one. I won't deny that your program might grow despite its shaky foundation. Knowing you, it probably will. However, I'm not counting on happenstances. I'm betting on total community involvement. The process is the product, and the people are the process. The process is not, as you believe, a single program sporting two dozen classes. Community education is democracy in action. What's more, before I'm through I'll have every agency in the community working on program development. I may end up scheduling one class to every three of theirs, but we'll all be under the community education umbrella." Harvesty sighed.

Johnson stood up, pushing his chair away from the table. "I tell my people — 'Give me the enrollments and I'll give you a class!' " Johnson yawned, stretching his huge frame. "It was great seeing you again, Bob. I'd like to chat with you further, but I don't want to miss the next session." Johnson paused. Then looking down at the smaller man, he put out his hand. "You come up with those six new programs, and lunch is on me next time we meet." His handshake was firm, and the grin on his face affable.

Harvesty watched his friend move briskly out of the luncheon area, greeting everyone with a wave of his hand and with a smile as wide as a pumpkin's on Halloween eve. Then he, too, arose. As he walked slowly along the hotel corridor, he began to have doubts about his own philosophy. Perhaps Johnson had the right idea, and he was just chasing a rainbow. He shrugged his shoulders, feeling a sudden chill creep up his back. Only time will tell, he thought!

## QUESTIONS

1. The case takes place at a regional seminar for community education coordinators. What is the purpose of a regional seminar?

2. Describe the leadership styles of the two community education directors.

3. Compare the philosophies of the key characters. Which of the two philosophies speaks to the value of building coordinated efforts in the community? Why are coordinated efforts important?

4. Should Johnson decide to expand his program to include other agencies? If so, what obstacles does he now have to overcome? Explain.

5. In including agencies in his community education projects, what risks are involved for Harvesty?

6. What is the difference between a director and a coordinator?

7. Cite the advantages of agency involvement. Discuss the over-

lapping and duplication of services, finances, and human resources.

8. "Process is only a vehicle to arrive at a program. It is not an end
in itself. If you can anticipate needs, you can virtually do away
with process." Write your reaction to this statement. Does
Johnson have the proper understanding of process? Explain.

9. "The process is the product and the people are the process."
Agree or disagree with this statement. Support and clarify your
answer.

10. How much time should be spent involving agencies and organizations in community education? What are some of the dangers
of overextended involvement? How should the community education director schedule his time?

11. Explain the function and purpose of a community resource
profile.

## ACTIVITIES

1. List some obvious voids of process in Johnson's community education program. How critical are these voids?

2. Role play a casual meeting between Johnson and Harvesty a year
later and have each man discuss the progress of his project.

3. List some major concerns why organizations and agencies might
be reluctant to join community education in the initial phase of
development.

4. Conduct a community resource profile with the major agencies
operating in your community and summarize your findings.

5. Collect community resource profile data and develop the data for
distribution to local agencies that took part in the community
resource profile.

6. Arrange a meeting with a representative of an agency that participated in the community resource profile and interpret your
findings to him.

CASE #12

## THE MUDDLED MEETING

The Tarrington School District's community education project was moving bumpily along according to schedule under the energetic direction of John Zale, a thirty-five year old junior high school industrial arts teacher. New to community education and still very much involved in the teaching of three shop classes at the Nathan Hadderman Junior High School, Zale had few moments to call his own and almost none which he shared with his family. Lately, his wife Susan and his two children, Joseph and Peter, rarely saw him, save at bedtime, when he would send his youngsters scampering off to their rooms with either a quick kiss on the cheek or a growl, depending on the nature of his day. When he was in a bad mood, Mrs. Zale quickly trailed after her children. When he was in a good mood, she listened to her husband recount his day's activities until her drooping eyelids closed and she fell asleep in an oversize stuffed chair. Since his good moods became increasingly infrequent, she generally retired early.

Tonight Zale was meeting his community-chosen advisory council for the second time. In responding to a community education survey conducted by Zale, Tarrington residents had been asked to name three persons whom they would want to represent them on a community advisory council. From these nominations representatives had been selected by the following criteria: geographic, ethnic, economic, and sex. As soon as the selection process was completed, Zale had sent letters of congratulations to the nominees. The letters not only contained an explanation of how they had been chosen, but also requested their presence at an upcoming information meeting.

Zale's initial presentation to the six nominees had been brief, lasting little more than an hour. During that time he had delivered a short lecture, shown a film, and distributed a few handouts, which enumerated the advantages of community education and illustrated programs of nearby districts. At the conclusion of the session, the nominees had been instructed to return the following week to discuss after careful deliberation what they had seen, heard, and would eventually read. At the next meeting questions would be invited from the small group of participants, and the unique advantages of the project for the Tarryington community would be explored. The group had left somewhat dazed by the presentation. Had they been asked to stay, at least half of them would have volunteered; for they were anxious to learn more about community education.

When the second meeting began, Zale, once again, went over the community education concept. While he did not want to belabor the points he had made earlier, he did want to make sure everyone had a clear understanding of community education.

Thirty minutes after the meeting had commenced in the high school classroom, he asked for responses from the group. They were ready, he was convinced, to determine their role in the program. The first member of the council to speak was Eldon Slattery, a dour-faced accountant, who had five children in the school system.

"Mr. Zale," said the balding little man, "if the project isn't going to cost the district any more money, I'm all for it. Unfortunately, my business, being what it is, keeps me out at night a good deal working with clients. I'm afraid I can't attend many sessions. But if you keep me posted with the minutes of each meeting, I'll try to do what I can. Mind you, I can't promise anything."

Zale smiled graciously at the accountant, who was sneaking a look at his watch. "I appreciate your kind offer to help, Mr. Slattery. Perhaps we can work the meetings around your busy schedule, if you can give us advance notice." Mr. Slattery grunted his satisfaction.

Doris Darby, the wife of a retired druggist, who was at fifty-five an active member of at least a dozen community associations, brandished her spindly arm in the air like a sword.

"What I'd like to know," said Mrs. Darby, raising her voice, "is what this program is going to do for the senior citizens of the community. What I have heard so far doesn't impress me one iota." Her steel gray eyes glared at Zale as she waited for an answer.

Before Zale could answer Mrs. Darby, Paul Jones, representing the black population in the community interjected. "Jobs — that's what my people need. This whole program sounds like recreation and play. I didn't hear anything said about how the program is going to meet the needs of the growing number of unemployed workers in this community." He finished with a scowl that made Zale shiver.

"A point well-taken, Mr. Jones," said Zale, "but one we as a group intend to investigate during our future meetings. We will have industrial tie-ins, you know. But we need your assistance every step of the way." Zale tugged at his collar and snapped a button off.

Dianne Rogers, a professor of sociology at Tarrington State University and a leader of the women's liberation movement in the community, stood up to address the group.

"I am, indeed, happy to serve my constituents. There are questions that have long gone unanswered in the community, questions which must be answered if our schools are ever to progress. It's about time we eliminated sexual discrimination from our textbooks and from our curricula. What's more, I would like to know why Tarrington has no women administrators in the district." Two members of the group clapped their hands as Dr. Rogers sat down.

Time was ticking away much too slowly for Zale. He desperately wanted the hour hand on his watch to touch nine so he could disperse the group. The literature he had read on community education had not prepared him for this kind of meeting, neither had his brief training stint at the Regional Community Education Center.

"What I'd like to know, Mr. Zale," groaned Manuel Peraz, the proprietor of Tarrington's leading restaurant, "is why you aren't giving us a little more direction. If I ran my business this way, I'd never make a dollar. If we're going to do anything, let's get started. I don't have all night to waste." Peraz cracked his huge knuckles, waiting for a reply.

"What we need," declared Mrs. Gregory Tillit, III, the wife of a prominent real estate broker, "is a big and exciting program. I'd like to teach a course in comparative literature; and I've already asked my daughter Jane to teach a baton-twirling class." Her eyes swept across the faces of the small group, stopping only to make a direct contact with the eyes of Zale. "Everybody will just love her. She is so professional. I think we should all teach something. That's what I call action."

"I am quite willing to teach a course in sexual discrimination," said Dr. Rogers. "The community is certainly in need of one."

"I don't have any time to teach courses," said Slattery irritably. "I think we're getting off to a bad start. I was under the impression that the teaching would be done by school personnel." His glasses slid to the edge of his perspiring nose as he shook his head in disgust.

Peraz was quick to admit that he also had no intention of going into a classroom. But no one paid any attention to him. They were too busy arguing among themselves about what the group should be doing.

At a quarter past nine Zale suggested that the meeting be adjourned, but only Mr. Slattery left. The others remained until ten, at which time the janitor inquired how much longer the group would be using the classroom. When Zale said he did not know, the group, as if by magic, filtered into the corridor to continue the discussion.

Zale tried to shake each representative's hand while the group moved out of the building and into the parking lot. After two unsuccessful tries, he gave up in despair. As they departed, he shouted that he would be contacting them again shortly.

Climbing into his car, Zale scratched his head in utter disbelief. "What have I gotten myself into?" he mumbled to himself. Trying to determine a future course of action, he drove slowly homeward.

## QUESTIONS

1. Discuss the early indications that Zale was going to encounter difficulty in developing the Tarrington community education program.

2. Is Zale's home life typical of people in community education? Discuss some of the problems and possible solutions that could overcome this occupational hazard.

3. Cite some problems encountered by Zale in the selection and training of the community advisory council.

4. Was Zale's advisory council truly advisory and did the group adequately represent a cross-section of Tarrington's citizens?

5. Discuss the difference between advisory and community councils. Outline the function of each.

6. At what point is the development of an advisory council feasible? Was Tarrington ready for one? Explain.

7. What should be Zale's next step with the advisory council? Outline a brief timetable and agenda for the next three meetings.

## ACTIVITIES

1. Brainstorm a list of community members who should be included on an advisory council.

2. Develop a presentation that Zale should have given to the newly formed advisory council.

3. Divide the class into small groups to develop the agenda item in question 2. Include resource material and content areas.

4. List each statement made by advisory council members that was

threatening to Zale. Role play each encounter and provide a more in-depth answer to each question.

5.  Role play Zale's next meeting with his advisory council, assuming that he had been given some technical assistance on how to solve his leadership problem.

## ANNOTATED READINGS

Berridge, Robert I. *The Community Education Handbook,* Midland, Michigan: Pendell Publishing Company, 1973. Chapter VI, Coordinating Community Resources; Chapter VIII, Community Councils. The author discusses the use of a community resource profile. While everyone agrees that all resources must be coordinated, the task of coordination is generally difficult to accomplish. The establishment of community councils is also discussed.

Burden, Larry, and Whitt, Robert L. *The Community School Principal,* Midland, Michigan: Pendell Publishing Company, 1973, (pp. 184-204). Three models depict community agency involvement in the school. Included is the Charrette Model for coordinating community efforts to attain positive school-community relationships.

Giles, Floyd K. "City Recreation Is More Involved Than Ever," *Community Education Journal,* Volume II, No. 4, August 1972, (pp. 34-39). The director of parks and recreation for Provo, Utah, describes the unification of the school and the city in a coordinated community education effort. Shown are benefits accrued by each governmental unit and the taxpayer.

Heimstra, Roger. *The Educative Community: Linking the Community, School and Family,* Lincoln, Nebraska: Professional Educators Publications, Inc., 1972. Chapter V, Community Coordination and Cooperation. The school and the community must cooperate with each other. Coordinated community programs and planning efforts are necessary to stimulate both educational and economic development. To attain this level of coordination, the author recommends the establishment of a central coordinating agency and describes its function. Before educators set out to coordinate the community, they must coordinate their educational program.

Hickey, Howard W., and Van Voorhees, Curtis. *The Role of the School in Community Education,* Midland, Michigan: Pendell Publishing Company, 1969. Chapter V, Community Schools: Their Relationship to Community Agencies, written by Arden Moon. The author presents a rationale for cooperative efforts in the community process. He lists possible areas of cooperation and techniques which might be employed by the community school director to bring about these efforts.

Kerensky, V. M., and Melby, Ernest O. *Education II — The Social Imperative,* Midland, Michigan: Pendell Publishing Company, 1971, (pp. 155-178). The authors, stressing a new theory and practice for educators, build a case for total community involvement in the educational system. In doing so, they draw upon John Gardner's beehive model for support. This model generally states that industry, government, and education, now functioning in isolation, must get together again to serve the large number of helpless people in society.

McNeill, David W. "The Community School Council — A Cooperative Effort," *Community Education Journal,* Volume I, No. 2, May 1971, (pp. 48-49). The author describes a community-wide council, first as an organizational model and then as an operational model.

Minzey, Jack, and LeTarte, Clyde E. *From Program to Process*, Midland, Michigan: Pendell Publishing Company, 1972, (pp. 63-77). The authors present a detailed discussion for establishing a community advisory council, which encompasses number, representation, and function. Included in their discussion is a method of conducting a needs assessment to coordinate existing community efforts.

Nierman, Wayne. "T. Wendell Williams Community Education Center for Coordination of Community Resources," *Community Education Journal*, Volume II, No. 1, February 1972, (pp. 45-49). The cooperative planning and construction of a facility to enhance cooperative efforts of agencies and organizations is described in depth as the story of the T. Wendell Williams Center unfolds. In addition to background information concerning the formulation of the project, pictures and architectural drawings are included.

Seay, Maurice F., and Associates. *Community Education: A Developing Concept*, Midland, Michigan: Pendell Publishing Company, 1974, (pp. 171-186). Parson, taking an in-depth look at the role, function, and power of a community council, deals with many specific aspects of community councils.

Stark, Stephen L. "Community Education — Coordination and Cooperation," *Leisure Today*, April 1974, (p. 10). The article presents a summary of cooperative programs, along with the rationale and support for building a unified effort in the community when developing a comprehensive community education program.

Totten, Fred. *The Power of Community Education*, Midland, Michigan: Pendell Publishing Company, 1970, (pp. 27-85). This section deals with many areas where involvement and cooperation are possible between school and community. These areas include social problems, crime prevention, and improving attitudes of children toward the school. Presented is a program description of how the school and community can jointly build programs for better living.

Whitt, Robert L. *A Handbook for the Community School Director*, Midland, Michigan: Pendell Publishing Company, 1971, (p. 57). The establishment and use of a community bulletin board is shown as an awareness tool to list classes and to publicize the coordinated efforts of many agencies. Board construction is explained. A list of Do's and Don'ts is included for the community educator.

# CHAPTER 5 Developing Policies and Procedures

Critical to the success of any community education program are operational policies and procedures that are compatible with the community education philosophy. The traditional operational policies and procedures that govern the normal school day quickly become obsolete for the evening use of public school facilities. Because the school takes on a new purpose and function in the evening hours, a new set of policies and procedures must be developed for a smooth transition from day to night use.

Many potentially good community education programs encounter operational difficulties or cease to exist because the school system has no policy for the extended use of its facilities. Before the first program is scheduled, it is essential to have in writing a clearly defined policy on building use. This policy should be drawn up by the community education director with the assistance of the business manager, principals, teachers, and custodians. Any proposed policy is, of course, subject to board review and action before it can be implemented. Under the auspices of board and superintendent and with the support of all who helped to develop the policy, the community education director may proceed to operationalize his program with confidence.

Community education is not restricted, however, to public school facilities. For example, churches, club rooms, and organizational facilities are available for expanded community education programs. Used extensively, these facilities are likely to engender the same kind of operational problems that emerge in the schools. Well-defined building policies are, therefore, as important in these facilities as they are in the schools. In the absence of such policies, community education cannot be expected to function effectively. To illustrate a few of the many problems that deal with policy, the following cases are presented.

The first case, in focusing upon the age-old problem of building security during evening hours, raises several questions. Who, for example, is responsible for overall building security? Does the custodian or the community education director lock the doors after programs conclude? When special functions, such as dances, are held, what precautions should be taken and by whom? And finally, how many doors and hallways should be accessible to the public after regular school activities cease?

A lack of communication constitutes the major problem in the second case, where policies and procedures that enhance community education are disregarded by a top school official. The seriousness of the situation becomes evident when the assistant superintendent of business and the community education director independently schedule building activities. The chaotic result is two activities scheduled for the same night. Complicating the situation further is the fact that the two men have different philosophies regarding building use. Whereas the community education director believes that school facilities should be made available for community activities at no cost to participants, the assistant superintendent of business demands that a fee be charged whenever buildings are used by the public.

In the third case custodial problems receive primary consideration. Simple everyday operational problems are allowed to overshadow the merits of a community education program. When this happens, programs become subordinate to housekeeping chores and maintenance emerges as a yardstick for determining the success of a community education program.

The well-prepared community education director is fully aware of policy pitfalls and, through early and extensive planning, takes every precaution to avoid them. In the final analysis, the success of a community education program depends upon policies which facilitate and guide the implementation of the full-utilization concept.

CASE #13

## A BREACH OF SECURITY

Del Lambert climbed into bed exhausted. He wasn't even tempted to steal a glance at the television guide to see what the late show had to offer. Tonight his love of sleep outweighed his ardor for the movies. It had been a hectic day at the community education project. The directorship he had accepted two months earlier was wearing him thin. By eleven he was sound asleep.

Thirty minutes later his wife Myrna was shaking his shoulder. He awoke, startled. "What's wrong?" he mumbled. His tongue was thick and his throat dry. "What happened?" He rubbed his eyes to see his wife.

"Superintendent Thompson is on the phone," she said, raising the volume of her voice as she continued to talk. "It's urgent."

"Urgent," he groaned, reaching for his slippers. "I don't understand." He staggered to the living room, shaking his head and blinking his eyes as he closed the distance between the phone and himself. "This is Del Lambert," he said weakly into the receiver. He could hear the voice of the superintendent only vaguely. There seemed to be a lot of noise in the background.

"Del, I don't have time for an elaborate explanation of why I called. I want you to get down to the high school as fast as you can. There's been trouble here. In fact, the police are in the building right now." The phone clicked.

Lambert stubbed his toe against a large coffee table and screamed in pain and anger as he dressed. All the way to the car the pain continued. When his anger subsided, fear took hold of him. He was a curious mixture of awe and consternation when he entered the building.

Superintendent Thompson met him at the other side of the glass door. "A gang of hoodlums were caught roaming around the building tonight. They've broken desks, audio-visual equipment, and office furniture. Lockers have been forced open, and books and papers are scattered throughout the corridors. I think they even had some kind of brawl on the second floor. The school is a mess." Thompson rubbed his forehead. He had a splitting headache. "Del, did you lock this building tonight?"

Thompson waited for an answer, watching the other man's eyes.

"I thought I did. I was so busy this evening running around the building that I might very well have overlooked locking up the building." Lambert fingered the keys in his pocket. "What does the janitor say?"

"Ed says the right wing of the building was wide open. What I can't understand is why." Thompson was perspiring in the cool building. "Aren't you restricting use of the facility to the left wing?"

"I've been opening all the entrances to the building to facilitate access on these cold fall evenings." Lambert wrung his hands. "I never expected anything like this. It's incredible!"

"Ed tells me that many of the windows were open in the left wing." Thompson moved over to the wall to lean against it. "How they got open I don't know, and neither does Ed."

"Where was the janitor when all this happened?" Lambert said angrily.

"In the rear of the building getting ready to go home. When he heard the noise, he called the police. Lucky for us he hadn't left. No telling what else might have occurred."

Officer Johnson walked over to the two men. "Everything seems to be under control now, Mr. Thompson. We've got all the kids out of the building. They were certainly having a field day with school property." The officer whistled under his breath.

"Thank you very much Officer Johnson," said Thompson, solemnly. "I truly appreciate the efforts of your department and especially your own, of course." The bushy-haired superintendent with gray sideburns shook hands with Officer Johnson.

After the officer had gone, Thompson and Lambert closed and locked every window in the building. Next they secured the doors. Before they parted it was two a.m. As Lambert stuck the keys of the building back into his pocket, Thompson lightly grasped his wrist. "Del," he said firmly, "don't ever let his happen again."

Lambert didn't fall asleep until four a.m. He kept thinking about his carelessness. Finally, when he had sufficiently reassured himself that it would never happen again, he slept soundly.

Three weeks later, Del Lambert arranged with a committee of students to hold a Teen Dance at the local junior high before the school closed for yuletide festivities. The first problem Lambert encountered was a lack of chaperones. He was able to get two teachers and wanted five. It was going to be a big crowd. It was open to every junior high school student in the community. Two parents volunteered, but at the last minute both were unable to come because of other pressing engagements. To help her husband, Mrs. Lambert consented to replace one of the missing parents. And the dance went ahead on schedule.

The Teen Dance was held on the Friday before the holidays commenced. By seven, half the teen population of Meredith was tracking snow into the building. To Mrs. Lambert some of them looked pretty old for junior high school students; and she passed this observation on to her husband. Mrs. Gregory, one of the two other chaperones, having made a similar judgment, approached Lambert on the same matter. She thought that at least one of the so-called boys looked older than Lambert, whom she knew to be close to thirty. Dismissing the concerns of his wife and Mrs. Gregory with a flick of his wrist, Lambert went back to amusing the teenagers who had been keeping him company.

The dance started smoothly at seven p.m. with Mr. and Mrs. Lambert joining in on the first dance; by eight, however, a number of unexpected developments had occurred. Mr. Tosby, the only other male chaperone, reported to Lambert that several of the students were staggering around the building, displaying their affection for each other in a rather uninhibited manner. They were obviously drunk said Tosby because one of the boys reeked of beer. At eight-thirty, there was a disturbance in the girls' restroom. When Mrs. Gregory checked it out, she found a teenaged girl sprawled out on the lavatory floor. She had apparently fainted after indulging excessively in alcoholic beverages. By nine, large numbers of teenagers were roaming the building. Others left for the parking lots to pile into their cars. Motors could be heard racing around at high speed, with tires screeching through the snow patched asphalt.

Eventually a fight broke out between two boys and, encouraged, others joined in the fracus. While one of the chaperones ran to the phone booth to call the police, another reported that a group of teenagers was smoking marijuana in the administrative suite of the building.

Officer Johnson, accompanied by his partner, Officer Darnell, promptly arrived in a screaming squad car. "Having trouble again, Mr. Lambert," Officer Johnson said politely.

"Yes, I am," said Lambert, "And I'm very happy to see you." There was a hard knot in Lambert's stomach.

In an hour most of the students were back in their homes. Alerted to the problem, a throng of parents had appeared on the scene to remove their children from what one parent had labeled "a sordid mess." Most withheld their comments, some with the expressed purpose of giving Superintendent Thompson a piece of their minds. One parent had said, while trying to contain his fury, "If this is community education, we don't want any part of it."

Lambert was seriously ill by the time he reached home. He, too, had changed his feelings about community education. Lying in the dark in his living room, long after his wife had gone to bed, he thought about what he would say to Superintendent Thompson when the call came.

And come it would, he was absolutely sure!

## QUESTIONS

1. Do you believe that Del Lambert should be held responsible for locking up the building?

2. What was the janitor's responsibility in maintaining building security?

3. Who was held responsible for the vandalism, and why?

4. What indication was there in the case that a poor relationship existed between Lambert and the custodian?

5. Discuss your feelings about using the police to handle school problems in the evening program.

6. What might be some positive uses of police in the community school program?

7. When Lambert scheduled the school dance, what mistakes did he make in handling building security and in controlling the dance?

8. What policies might Lambert have devised to be assured that only junior high school students were admitted to the dance?

9. Do you think a uniformed policeman should be used to assist chaperones at a junior high school dance? Explain your position.

10. List some of the security measures that Lambert had neglected to take in operating his community education program.

## ACTIVITIES

1. Develop a policy concerning opening and closing a community school building at night; identify the role of the community school director and the janitor in implementing this policy.

2. Write a policy for conducting a teen dance in a community

school, and outline the roles and duties of all supervisory personnel.

3. List the critical areas to be supervised in the building and on the grounds during a school dance.

4. As a group project, develop a teen code of ethics for responsibility and behavior during a school-sponsored dance. Also, list punitive measures to be taken for negative behavior, such as drinking, smoking, and fighting.

5. Role play the meeting between Del Lambert and Superintendent Thompson after the trouble at the school dance.

**CASE #14**

## A LACK OF POLICY

It was an unusually warm Midwestern October, and the early morning sun shone brightly. The leaves clung tenaciously to the trees, and the graying grass was recapturing some of its verdant luxuriousness. It was forecasted that the temperature would climb into the eighties for the third day.

Most of the Central City High School students stepped off the school bus, wearing neither coat nor jacket. There were a few who wore sweaters. Occasionally, a student could be seen promenading into the building with uprolled sleeves. Indian summer had arrived, and everyone appeared to be taking advantage of it.

For Joe Weston, the community education project director, it was a glorious day. Everything seemed to be going perfectly for him. Fifteen courses had been scheduled, and all were filled to capacity. Through conversations held with instructors and students, Weston had learned that a climate of general satisfaction prevailed. Furthermore, not only was the program meeting the expectations of both groups, it was also gaining the unanimous approval of the superintendent and board. Despite their initial skepticism about whether the program could succeed, he had won them strongly over to his side.

Weston did not profess to be a community education expert. His training had been slight — a course in community education and a workshop at a community education training center, where he and a board member had spent a week. As far as experience went, he had none. What he did have, however, was an overwhelming belief in the community education concept.

Weston had been a guidance counselor for twenty years in the same school, and he knew his community well. Until he was introduced to community education, he had never given much thought to the full-school utilization concept. Now he espoused it daily.

When the phone rang, Weston was writing in his ledger the names of two more community service clubs that wanted to use the cafeteria for special activities. While he scheduled the use of the cafeteria, he removed the phone from its cradle and lifted it to his ear.

"Mr. Weston," a soft feminine voice said, "Mr. Sullivan would like to speak to you."

"Good morning, Doris," said Weston, completing his notes, "How are things at central office?"

"A little hectic, Joe," she said taking a deep breath, "I better put you through to Mr. Sullivan." The line clicked.

"That you, Joe," said the assistant superintendent of business. It was more a statement than a question.

"Good morning, Mr. Sullivan. How are you today?" Weston doodled while he talked.

"Skip the amenities, Joe," grumbled Sullivan. "We've got real problems."

"Problems?" Weston put his pen down.

"What's this I hear about your letting all the service clubs in the community use our facilities for nothing."

"What's wrong with that? The building belongs to them, too. They pay taxes." Weston paled. There was a quiver in his voice.

Sullivan roared. "Joe, they're making money on these deals. The last club that used our gymnasium netted two hundred dollars profit. The members are bragging about it all over town; and now every other club in the community wants to use the school for fund raising activities." The assistant superintendent paused. "Are you with me, Joe?"

The line was silent. Then Weston groaned. "Full-school utilization is part and parcel of the community education concept. Without it, my program may very well go down the drain. We've never had so much activity in the school, not in the past twenty years." Weston glanced at the sun peering through his window and blinked in annoyance.

"You're telling me. I've been hearing all about it from our custodial staff," Sullivan panted. "You can't expect them to do all that extra work. By renting the facility, we can pay for any additional help we need. The rent also pays for wear and tear on the building. That's been my rule for a long time, and it's a sound one!"

"But . . . " gulped Weston, before he was cut off.

"No but's, Joe," yelled Sullivan. "I don't want you scheduling that building without my approval. And all prior commitments are off." The phone slammed in Weston's ear.

Weston sat hunched over his desk, his head propped up on his elbows. For an hour he brooded. He had neither the nerve nor the desire to cancel the commitments he had made. Ultimately, he decided that he would wait until Wednesday. Today was Monday, and there was nothing scheduled until then. He had to have more time to prepare the argument that he would present to the superintendent. He had to calculate costs. But more important, the senior citizens' dance would be held in the gymnasium Wednesday, an event that he felt obliged to make a success. He was seeking greater involvement from them in the project. Thus far their participation had been relatively meager.

Wednesday evening it was Weston's intention to be on hand when the senior citizens arrived at seven, but the problem of a last minute class cancellation detained him at the other end of the building. As soon as he dismissed the students, he hurried to the gymnasium to welcome the senior citizens. He was eager to see the expressions on their faces when they saw how attractively the gym had been decorated by the steering committee. It would be a gala festivity, he thought; one they would long remember.

A large crowd of people stood outside the gymnasium, about half of whom were teenagers. They were carrying athletic bags with St. Joseph High School written on them. Meanwhile, filtering out of the gymnasium were at least two dozen gray-haired men and women. Evicting them was the chief custodian. That the senior citizens were bewildered was quite apparent. Weston was equally perplexed; he couldn't imagine what had happened. There had been no other group activity scheduled for Wednesday.

"Mr. Teat," he said loudly, "what is the meaning of this?" The custodians were busy ripping down the decorations. "The gymnasium has been scheduled for a dance this evening." One of the custodians was dragging a mat into the center of the gym.

"All I know is that there's a gymnastic event scheduled here tonight, and I only got twenty minutes to move a ton of equipment." Mr. Teat shrugged his shoulders and walked away.

"I told you there was a dance tonight," Weston shouted, his face was scarlet. "If I told you once, I told you twenty times." Weston felt like hitting the janitor.

"That was before Mr. Sullivan spoke to you," Mr. Teat said nonchalantly.

"How do you know he spoke to me?" exploded the community education director. "What he says to me is none of your business."

"I report to Mr. Sullivan, not to you." The custodian clenched his fists. "What he says goes!" The two men glared at each other.

"There'll be no gymnastics event here tonight," said Weston.

"Young man," said a voice behind him. "We've rented the use of the facility."

Weston turned toward the voice. "I'm sorry, Father," he said apologetically, "I scheduled the gym for this dance weeks ago."

"I don't understand," said the priest.

"I'm going to call Mr. Sullivan," said Mr. Teat, taking huge strides across the gymnasium. "He'll straighten this mess out."

"And I'm calling the superintendent," yelled Weston, feeling his legs suddenly grow weak. Moving slowly along the corridor toward his office he almost detoured into the parking lot.

As he dialed the superintendent's home number, Weston wondered what he was going to say to his superior. The thoughts that whirled around in his head frightened him. He had directly disobeyed one superordinate and purposely withheld a pressing problem from another. He had jeopardized school-community relations and had practically fought with the janitor. On top of all that, he was presently demanding a showdown that could easily eradicate twenty years of outstanding service to the district.

When he heard the superintendent's voice on the other end of the line, he was, at first, speechless. Then his words began to flow.

## QUESTIONS

1. What was the first indication that Weston and the assistant superintendent of business had communication problems?

2. When should a service club be allowed to profit from the free use of school facilities?

3. What proof is there that Mr. Sullivan hadn't yet accepted the community education program in the district?

4. "I don't want you scheduling that building without my approval!" If you were Weston, how would you have reacted to this statement? What was Weston's reaction?

5. How did Weston's procrastinations contribute to the magnitude of his problem? What action should he have taken on Monday?

6. Describe the relationship that existed between Weston and the custodial staff.

7. How could the overscheduling of the gymnasium have been avoided?

8. "I report to Mr. Sullivan, not to you." What's wrong with this type of administration in a community education program?

9. How could Weston have resolved his problem without calling

the superintendent?

10. Why should Weston be required to take orders from Mr. Sullivan? Where should each man be in the school district's organizational chart?

### ACTIVITIES

1. Write a facility-use policy to be adopted by the board of education in Central City.

2. Develop a policy that would permit organizations and clubs to use a facility for profit.

3. Role play a meeting between Weston and Sullivan to establish a good working relationship between the two men.

4. Develop a flow chart and rationale showing the role of the community education director, business manager, and custodial staff.

5. Write up a building-use policy that would prevent two groups from being scheduled in the facility at the same time.

6. Role play the phone conversation between Weston and the superintendent during the showdown.

**CASE #15**

## TO TOUCH A PRINCIPAL

The remark that Superintendent Carl Roderick had made about com-. munity education continued to pain Paul Layton as he drove away from the administration building. To Layton, the director of community education in the Wentworth Independent School District, Roderick had said only minutes ago, "It seemed like a good idea at the time, but now I'm not so sure."

Layton was on his way to Gifford High School to see what all the trouble was about. Apparently, Roderick was reluctant to confront the principal of Gifford on the issue of community education or, for that matter, on any other issue. Bill Davis, Gifford's principal, had twenty-five years of seniority behind him; Roderick was just beginning his second year in the district. Davis had, in fact, been offered the superintendency but turned it down, preferring to remain at Gifford, where all his professional life had been spent, for the most part, quite happily.

Davis was proud of his staff. Once they were hired, few teachers ever left Gifford for other teaching positions. Davis was admired by almost everyone who worked for him, and to his followers he gave his unqualified support. Davis was also extremely proud of his student body, which was comprised of youngsters he had watched grow up in a community he had always known as home. Indeed, many of the students that now attended Gifford were the children of his former students, all of whom respected him highly as an educator and a leading citizen. And last but not least, Davis was proud of his school. Well-known for its cleanliness and "newness" even after ten years of use, it epitomized the custodial function.

Paul Layton considered all these facts carefully as he maneuvered his car along the winding road which led to the high school. He considered, as well, what he thought to be the salient part of his discussion with Superintendent Roderick.

In what he recollected to be a rather cautious and uncertain tone of voice, Roderick had said, "Believe me, I want the program; so do many others in the community. But, as you know, I have been getting many complaints lately from Principal Davis; the last one is not thirty minutes old. I want the matter straightened out as quickly as possible. I respect Davis very much. He's a fine administrator. Seldom complains, as a matter of fact. A most helpful person, whose support we obviously need to ensure the program's success. I suggest you get together with him before this thing explodes. A morale problem I don't need — nor want!"

To this, Layton had replied half-heartedly. "I'll do my best; unfortunately, he hasn't been very supportive since the program began three months ago. And whatever's bothering him now is probably no different from what has been bothering him all along." Layton had ended with a sigh.

"I'd go over with you;" Roderick had said, moving over to the pile of paper on his desk, "however, with the upcoming budget already plainly in view, I don't have a moment to spare away from my data collections. I might add," he had paused to say, his voice faltering, "that I received a couple of complaints from teachers this morning, too. Both good people. Got me seriously thinking about the merits of the program." Then he had raised his voice to say, as if dismissing, for a time, the implications of the calls, "I think you better go now. Get the whole story. And when you return, we'll sit down and discuss what needs to be done."

But Layton had not been willing to be dismissed without some kind of clarification on the nature of the complaints.

"What were the specific complaints of the teachers?" Layton had asked rather authoritatively. "If I am going to deal with this problem effectively, I think I ought to know." While he had waited for an answer, his shoulders came erect.

Roderick had sat down before he made any effort to answer the younger man. Then he had said, gripping the arms of his swivel chair in an impatient gesture, "One reported missing supplies — a few pencils, a ruler, and, I believe, a chalkboard eraser; the other complained about an open window and rain on the floor and alluded to the potential hazard inherent in the situation."

"Why did they call you?" Layton had asked almost involuntarily, propelled once again by the fervor of his commitment to the program. "Why not me? That's what I'm here for, isn't it? Instead, they by-pass me every time."

"In answer to your first question," Roderick had said, his voice quavering, "I simply don't know. Perhaps, it's because of their seniority. They've been around here a long time. In the past, they have called about other matters, so this case is not an isolated incident." Roderick had then stood up and led Layton to the door. Opening the door widely he had added, "Need I say their gripes are legitimate."

Layton entered the high school parking lot and parked in an area designated for faculty. Taking only a moment to lock his car, he moved briskly toward the front of the building. In the corridor outside the administrative suite, he returned the waves of several students whose parents were currently enrolled in community education classes.

Leaning over the long counter that separated visitors from office personnel, Layton asked, "Is Principal Davis in his office?"

Mrs. Bell responded to his inquiry almost before he had finished making it. "He's expecting you. Go right in!"

Layton extended his hand to Davis, and there it remained as if suspended in mid-air until he buried it in his pocket. While Layton blushed, Davis turned toward a large double window, hands clasped behind his back.

"I want you to know that I'm thoroughly dissatisfied with this program of *yours.*" Davis fumed. "It continues to cause me unnecessary grief."

"You seemed to be favorably inclined toward it the last time we talked, at least in the spirit of giving it a fair chance to succeed." Layton tried to catch the eyes of the principal as he turned to face him. Layton's forehead was wrinkled, his eyebrows raised.

Staring down at the tiled floor, the principal said, "I tried my best to help, but the program is destroying this school, not to mention the morale of the faculty."

Layton groaned. "What seems to be the problem?" — this time, he added in his thoughts.

"Look, I tolerated cigarette butts on the classroom floor. I even put up with chairs pushed all over the room, making it almost impossible for the custodial staff to clean, and with innumerable scuffed floors. But when windows and supplies are tampered with, I've just got to put my foot down." Davis paced the room, shaking his head in disgust.

Layton, now seated, said softly, "Tell me more about the supplies and windows."

"What is there to tell?" Davis almost yelled. "Supplies were missing, and windows were open, exposing the school to possible vandalism and to the inclemency of the weather. The room was a mess this morning."

"Why didn't the custodian close the window? Correct me if I'm wrong, but isn't he supposed to tidy up the rooms after classes are over?" Layton crossed one leg over the other when his shoe began to tap against the floor.

Davis, putting his hands on his hips, leaned over Layton, his face glowering. "Don't tell me what the custodian is supposed to do. He's got plenty to do ever since the school turned into an all night movie. I sympathize with him."

Layton redirected the conversation to the supply problem. There was no point in talking about the custodial function. He had listened to a similar diatribe at least a half dozen times before. The story was always the same — butts on floor; a discarded sandwich, perhaps; for certain, scuffed up floors; and, of course, the perennial problem of rearranged furniture. That's how it went — little molehills becoming horrendous mountains. "What about the supplies?"

Through clenched teeth, Davis said, "There were pencils missing from Miss Hornberry's desk. A ruler was stolen, and so was an eraser."

"Come on, stolen! That's a pretty harsh word. Aren't you exaggerating a little?" Layton sat on the edge of his chair. "Exactly how many pencils?"

"That's beside the point!" Davis said indignantly.

"Two, three, five, ten; tell me, how many?" His voice was a growl.

Instead of responding to the question, Davis changed the subject.

"I want you to know that the entry way to the building was a disgrace this morning. Butts all over the place. The grass was trampled. Those people just don't appreciate the value of school property. I think the only way to solve all our problems is to restrict your activities to a confined area, say, for example, the gymnasium. In my book, that is, in fact, the only answer!"

"The program can't function properly that way. It's got to have the free run of the facility so that offerings can be optimized. I need classrooms. I need shops. I can't be confined to the gymnasium. Can't you understand?" Layton suddenly felt sick. Failure was closing in on him in the form of Davis. He began to rise, only to slip back in his seat.

"Take it or leave it. Henceforth, I shall expect you to restrict your festivities to the gymnasium, where I imagine damage may be minimized." Davis' voice grated the air.

"I suggest we leave that decision up to Superintendent Roderick and the board of education." Layton stood up. The two men faced each other, standing almost nose to nose.

"I'm sure they will agree with me," sneered the principal. "They always have. A report is already on its way to both the superintendent and the president of the board."

"Thanks for your time," said Layton sarcastically. Then in all sincerity, he added, "I only wish you could appreciate the good that this program is capable of doing for the people in this community. I only wish . . . " his words dangled in the air. With a splitting headache, Layton left the office of the principal.

Where did he go from here, he asked himself as he stood outside the building, staring off into space. Should he turn to the community for help? How much support could he expect from Roderick, who, himself, was in a precarious position? What about the board members who had been in favor of the program? All of these thoughts, and more, crossed his mind as a fresh breeze blew against his face; but no decision, aside from making his report to Roderick as quickly as possible, was immediately forthcoming.

## QUESTIONS

1. What alternatives were open to Paul Layton at the close of the case? Cite other possibilities, or strategies, not considered by him.

2. What assistance, if any, could Layton expect from Superintendent Roderick?

3. What was Superintendent Roderick's original position of community education? What indication is there that his present position reflects a somewhat altered perspective?

4. Why does Layton view Roderick's position as precarious?

5. How long has Roderick been superintendent of the Wentworth Independent School District?

6. Based on three months operation, is this a typical problem? If so, how could Layton have avoided the situation?

7. How does Principal Davis give strong evidence of being a formidable opponent in any future contest?

8. Why does Davis object to the community education program?

9. Why does Layton complain about having his activities restricted to the gymnasium?

10. What kind of administrator is Layton? Roderick? Davis? Classify, if possible, their leadership styles.

11. How is a measure of community education success revealed when Layton first enters the building?

12. What are Layton's chances of salvaging the community education program?

## ACTIVITIES

1.  Rewrite the ending of the case so that all issues are satisfactorily resolved.

2.  Reenact the ending of the case by assuming the roles of principal and community education director. Direct the new ending to an alternative conclusion.

3.  Role play the scene where Layton reports back to Superintendent Roderick.

4.  Arrange a three-way meeting of superintendent, principal, and community education director to resolve major differences.

5.  Should the problem be taken to status leaders in the community to obtain their support? Discuss the implications.

6.  Use brainstorming techniques to list alternatives which Layton may implement most advantageously.

7.  Use polling techniques on the class to determine whether Layton should continue to pursue his program objective.

8.  List the conditions underlying the major problem. Discuss in small groups how these conditions might be changed.

## ANNOTATED READINGS

Burden, Larry, and Whitt, Robert L. *The Community School Principal,* Midland, Michigan: Pendell Publishing Company, 1973, (pp. 149-168). The custodian is a key factor in successful community education administration. Whitt devotes an entire chapter to work schedules, job descriptions, inservice programs, and various forms of custodial problems and solutions.

Hickey, Howard W., and Van Voorhees, Curtis. *The Role of the School in Community Education,* Midland, Michigan: Pendell Publishing Company, 1969. Chapter IV, Community Schools: Their Administration, written by Clyde M. Campbell; Chapter IX, Community Schools: Physical Facilities, written by Charles G. Clark; Chapter X, A Community School: Day to Day Operations, written by P. Keith Gregg. The chapters deal with the difference between the community school and the traditional school. Philosophy, facility use, and scheduling of programs are discussed by the authors.

Minzey, Jack, and LeTarte, Clyde E. *From Program to Process,* Midland, Michigan: Pendell Publishing Company, 1972, (pp. 229-239). A problem faced daily by the community education director is the lack of proper facilities and policies governing the use of the facilities. Minzey and LeTarte, in this chapter, provide an insight into school-plant planning for immediate and future needs. The idea of adapting old facilities to meet the needs of new curriculums is discussed along with school-park sites, outside facilities, and joint usage of public and private facilities for community education programs.

Kirby, John T. "Community Use of School Facilities," *Community Education Journal,* Volume I, No. 2, May 1971, (pp. 14-15, 29). Inherent in the concept of community education is the assumption that community activities, educational, recreational or cultural, may take place on school premises. The author discusses the possibility of legal challenges to community education in the light of court cases and legal interpretations.

Whitt, Robert L. *A Handbook for the Community School Director,* Midland, Michigan: Pendell Publishing Company, 1971, (pp. 46-56). The program phase of community education is reviewed for enrichment activities, remedial activities, recreation activities, and special programs. Viewed as ways of attacking pressing social problems are guidance, health and police-liaison programs.

# CHAPTER 6 Financing Community Education

The single most crucial problem affecting the growth of community education across the country is financing the project. Most school boards will readily accept the philosophy of community education, but the true test of commitment comes from their willingness to finance its implementation. To say community education costs nothing is an unfair statement. To say it is very expensive is, again, a misinformed response. The fact is, community education does cost additional dollars that the school board must be ready to absorb in the very beginning of a project or at some point in the development of the program when soft monies disappear.

While the cost may be in-kind, indirect, or attached to another program budget, the fact remains that it will cost the district something. The cost is in direct proportion to the size of the program. Normally, at least one-half of the coordinator's salary is picked up by the local district. Some recreational help, generally part-time, and an office with a few supplies should also be provided by the local district. When the district provides utilities for extended school day use, the necessary commitments are complete for initiating a community education project.

The authors feel that through a moderate fee structure for classes and adequate involvement of agencies and organizations a very successful project can be developed. The secret in keeping the budget down is to keep outside assistance up. Through careful planning and involvement of all segments of community life, most communities are able to provide the financial resources necessary to run the program phase of community education.

Today, many districts receive some outside assistance to initiate their community education projects. This strategy is an excellent way to become involved in community education; however, to build the financial structure of a community education project on only soft money is to invite project failure. The authors feel that the true spirit of community education is attained when the project is funded by local dollars, regardless of how they are generated. Community participants become more supportive, more concerned and more involved when their local dollars are funding the program.

To illustrate some of the common pitfalls of financing community education, the following three case studies have been developed. A careful analysis of each will provide the student with some in-depth knowledge of contemporary problems affecting the expansion of community education.

The first case deals with the administrative responsibilities of the community education director when handling public school monies. The lack of policy governing collection, retention, and disbursement of monies collected through community education programs is highlighted in this case.

The dilemma that occurs when soft money is no longer available to fund a project is explained in the second case. Having ignored offerings of volunteer assistance and local financing in the early days of the project, the director is unprepared to sustain his project when outside monies are depleted. By this time, volunteers have lost their interest, and funds from prospective community sources have been withdrawn.

In case three, the question raised is whether or not a participant should pay to attend community education classes. The effect payment has on the attendance, commitment, and support of program participants is portrayed as the case progresses.

The authors trust that each student will gain from the cases a broader understanding of the importance of financial management. While an improper use of financial resources may not, in itself, constitute the only impediment in maintaining a successful community education program, it is most surely one that deserves the critical attention of the community educator.

**CASE #16**

## SELF-APPOINTED BUSINESS MANAGER

Arthur Gilman paced the floor of his living room while his wife Linda, ensconced on the divan, watched patiently.

"I lost everything," he kept repeating. He slammed the ball of his fist into an open hand. "Well, they won't catch me napping next time." Moaning, he said, "How do they expect me to build up my program if they take away my profits?"

Linda Gilman, knowing her husband expected no answer, remained silent. Having been married to him for fifteen years, she knew quite well that he never asked questions for which he did not have some kind of pat answer. Contrary opinions were generally refuted with a derisive laugh and the neat expression, "You don't understand." Arthur was a stubborn man, she reflected.

For fourteen years, Gilman had taught woodshop at Genoa High School. This year he was directing the district's newly initiated community education project, as well as teaching three classes in woodworking.

Gilman's entree into community education had been a booming success. This fall he had offered twelve courses, and several of them had doubled in anticipated enrollments. At the very least, there had been fifteen students in a class. By not limiting class size, Gilman had made a considerable profit. Unfortunately, the monetary gain he had realized after teacher salaries were deducted from the gross receipts was immediately absorbed by the school system.

Since no line item had ever been established in the school budget for community education funds, the business manager deposited the profits in the general fund, where they became inaccessible to Gilman. As a result, Gilman had, in a frenzy, vowed that he, alone, would handle, thereafter, the monies generated by the project.

Gilman labored to make the spring semester even better than the fall, and his toil was rewarded. Twenty courses carried with substantial overloads. Profits were higher than ever. In order to hold on to them, Gilman became his own business manager. He paid his overworked instructors their stipend in cash and tossed in a bonus to secure their continued allegiance. What was left he hid away in an old wooden cigar box which he kept in the bottom drawer of his desk. To avoid endless bookkeeping and a lot of unnecessary drudgery, he dispensed with the giving of receipts. The only registration record he kept was contained in the hasty scribbling of the pocket-sized looseleaf notebook he carried in his suit coat.

The second week of the spring semester he experienced his first business problem. A student who had been issued no receipt requested a refund. Because there was no checkmark next to the alleged registrant's name in his notebook, he was dubious about ever having collected the course fee. In good faith, however, he promptly issued a refund, withdrawing the money from his wooden cash register.

The fifth week he experienced an attendance problem. The instructors complained acrimoniously that their classes kept getting larger and that they were seeing strange faces each week. In an attempt to rectify the situation, he spent untold hours trying to decipher the hieroglyphics in his notebook, but all to no avail. Finally, he asked the instructors to bear with him, promising them that their patience would be rewarded shortly by the arrival of many of the instructional materials they had requested. Despite his abortive efforts, the situation somehow managed to take care of itself. For unexplained reasons, the supposed visitors began to disappear.

Toward the end of the semester, he was confronted with two other dilemmas. Not only was there one hundred dollars missing from his cigar box, but also he had lost or misplaced his registration notebook. The first problem he resolved by virtually tearing his desk apart. Beneath a sheaf of papers lay most of the missing bills. The balance, he was sure, he would find later; but he never did. Action succumbed to procrastination, and he stopped searching. The second problem was eliminated by purchasing a new notebook, which he completely filled with the names of students provided by his instructors.

About the middle of the summer, he was instructed to report immediately to the superintendent's office. There he encountered both the superintendent and the business manager. Before he spoke, the superintendent told Gilman to close the door. "Mr. Gilman," said Paul Taylor, the district's superintendent, shifting his eyes toward the business manager, "Mr. Jackson is a little troubled by the extent of your spending. And frankly, so am I."

Picking up the conversation, the business manager said, "You've been spending twice the capital outlay allotted by school district policy. Aren't you aware of the budgetary restrictions we have?"

"No, sir," said Gilman humbly.

"I supposed not," said Jackson, watching Gilman chew at his nails.

"I think you better bring all your records to Mr. Jackson *at once.*"

Superintendent Taylor tapped his foot against the floor.

"I want to see your credits, debits, and purchases for the past year. I also want to see the record of your instructors' salary withholdings," said Jackson sternly.

Gilman bent forward in his chair, burying his face in his hands, his elbows resting on his knees. "I didn't take out any withholding tax," mumbled Gilman into his hands.

"What!" shouted the superintendent. Gilman said nothing.

"I suggest you return immediately to the high school and pick up your records," said Jackson. "I'd like to review them now."

"Bring back your registration records, too," said the superintendent, frowning. "It's about time I saw what you've been doing over there."

"Yes, sir," said Gilman, rising weakly from his chair.

"Be back here in one hour," said the superintendent gruffly. "If I'm not here when you get here, I soon will be."

With his hand glued to his notebook, Gilman dashed out of the office. While he started his car, he wondered what kind of record he could make out of the scribblings in his notebook. He also wondered if he could locate in one hour all the orders and invoices he kept at work and home. At that moment, he was, indeed, sorry that he had ever assumed the role of business manager. He was even sorrier that he had ever left the class-room to direct the community education project. "What to do?" kept repeating over and over again in his mind.

## QUESTIONS

1. Discuss the theory of profits in a community education project. Why should profits never be viewed as the primary goal of a program?

2. What evidence is there in the case that Gilman may have some problems being a successful community education coordinator?

3. Did the business manager have a right to Gilman's profits? If so, describe how Gilman might have handled the situation more effectively.

4. Cite some reasons why Gilman should not handle the monies generated by the program.

5. List some problems Gilman might face in paying teachers directly out of the account he personally devised.

6. Describe Gilman's handling of registration records for community education classes and list some of the problems created by his inefficiency.

7. How supportive do you think the superintendent and business manager were of Gilman's community education program? Cite some examples.

8. Discuss whether or not the business manager had a sound program for handling the community education financial problems.

9. How was Gilman's inability to function as a business manager revealed in the case?

## ACTIVITIES

1. Develop a policy for handling school monies that are generated by a community education project. Outline possible ways of making funds accessible to Gilman in this policy.

2. Write a refund policy for a community education director to use when conducting a program where fees are charged.

3. Design a budget for a year's operation of a community education program and allocate appropriate expenditures.

4. List some services a good school district might provide in initiating a community education program.

5. Role play Gilman's return to the superintendent's office and list suggestions of how Gilman might get out of his dilemma.

**CASE #17**

## THE RECKONING

Under the direction of Leroy Van Fone, community education had a grand beginning in the Brunswick School District. It was like a bright star during its first year of operation, shining radiantly from one end of the city to the other in three different project sites.

With a federal grant of $80 thousand to spearhead his activities, Van Fone, an energetic middle-aged man, wasted no time in making a variety of course offerings available to an interested community. Within six weeks the robust Van Fone had hired two community education directors and commenced operations in three large secondary schools.

Acting as the district coordinator and operating, as well, the largest site of the three, Van Fone spent about a week brainstorming with his associates about the direction they would take, the needs of the community they would meet, and the kind of staffing they would require.

Since money was no problem, Van Fone decided early that courses would be offered at no expense to the public. Though he was not averse to the notion of using volunteers, he saw at this point little need for them. As long as funds were more than ample, he would postpone what he candidly admitted might be an eventual necessity. In the not too distant future, he would, however, develop a plan for their inclusion. Because of his decision he very politely refused several offers from some rather capable people who wished to volunteer their instructional services. Later he would regret that decision.

It took another two weeks for Van Fone to staff his program. To get the best qualified teachers, he offered salaries well above the normal pay scale. The inducement sent teachers scurrying to-and-fro across the city to participate. They were excited by the grandiose nature of the program called community education and dazzled by the three men who dashed in and out of buildings all day, sporting red blazers with open umbrellas embroidered under their lapel pockets. The teachers came in droves to enlist, needing no more than a welcoming nod to join the illustrious task force.

The same was true of the community. The media, television, radio, and newspaper, kept community education in the limelight for weeks.

The district newsletter bombarded the homes of the public. The staff bulletin kept the fires burning in the school. Students wrote about community education in their school newspapers. Every day, the public was made increasingly aware of the program's attributes.

Then the big day occurred, and the citizenry inundated the schools. It was a gala festivity. The schools had been decorated by a half dozen school organizations, some comprised of students, others parents. Bulletin boards were glowing, and displays were in great numbers. Teachers, dressed in their finest attire, greeted the crowd with warm handshakes and refreshments, and the programs skyrocketed into existence. The event was heralded as the birth of community education in Brunswick.

During that hectic period, Van Fone was invited to several luncheons, gave numerous speeches about the merits of community education, and turned down, as was his usual inclination, at least five offers from local industrialists to help finance the program. Van Fone wasn't worried about money with a second year of funding at another $80 thousand in the offing.

To each of his speaking engagements, Van Fone brought a sense of the drama. At times, he, in fact, overplayed his role, but always to the enjoyment of his audience. Van Fone's asset was, perhaps, being at home on any stage. Formerly a director of drama for the school district and a winner of many awards, he had gathered an impressive following over the decade of his employment with Brunswick. Now at forty-five, still relatively untouched by time, he was a strikingly handsome bachelor, who was reputed to be a supreme but gifted egoist with a flair for both the spectacular and the sublime.

Van Fone's office was said to be larger and better staffed than the superintendent's. His secretary, indeed, was paid better than any other secretary in the district. His two assistants did not fare badly either. They had new desks and an array of sparkling office equipment, freshly purchased and paid for in full. They were able to attend meetings, workshops, and the national convention on a budget that seemed like the legendary horn of plenty. Morale was further enhanced by the purchase of color television sets for the casual recreation of employes and participants. There appeared to be no end to the community education extravaganza.

The second year, community education lost much of its original luster. No longer glamorous and largely routinized, the programs in the three schools dwindled and so did the once laborious efforts of Van Fone and his subordinates. Van Fone yearned for the stage again, bit-acted quite frequently, and often disappeared for three or four evenings in a row. Lately, his speaking talents were seldom in demand, the interests of his staunch supporters having been diverted to new and more promising challenges.

There were moments when Van Fone seriously considered a dramatic comeback, but rarely did he implement any enterprising thoughts. One of his community education directors finally resigned to accept a principalship in a nearby district and the other fell into what appeared to be an irreversible slump.

On the second Monday in the month of February, Van Fone received a cordial phone call from Dr. Matlock, the superintendent of the district. The purpose of the call was to suggest that he and Van Fone meet the following afternoon to discuss the future of community education in Brunswick.

Van Fone was not unaccustomed to meeting with the superintendent. As a matter of fact, he did so quite often. Nevertheless, Van Fone was inordinately disturbed. He knew what was on the superintendent's mind. The federal funds were rapidly diminishing, and no new sources of funding were immediately evident to him.

Delaying the meeting until Friday, Van Fone spent the next three days contacting prospective program volunteers. All of the original volunteers, save one, were no longer interested in the community education project. After twelve hours of telephoning, he was able to produce only four more volunteers. People had apparently become indifferent to the project. His next strategy was to contact outside sources for possible funding, but this activity was curtailed considerably because he was also trying to spend time interviewing applicants for the vacant post of community education director.

Before driving down to the superintendent's office, Van Fone made an extensive list of goals, strategies, and possibilities for program funding and growth. It was more work than he had done in several weeks. He did not have much confidence in his suggestions, but they would have to suffice until better ones came along, from whom and where, he did not know.

As he sat down in a battered leather chair in Dr. Matlock's office, he made a mental wager with himself that his deepest fears would shortly be realized. Three minutes after social amenities were exchanged, he both won and lost his bet. Listening to the superintendent solemnly remind him that the federal grant was rapidly running out and ask how he intended to sustain the program, he repeatedly dropped his eyes to his lengthy list, hoping with each glance that his luck had not deserted him. In another minute he would have the answer. Regaining some of his former confidence, he mumbled to himself, "All the world's a stage."

## QUESTIONS

1.  Why was Van Fone not the right person to implement a community education program, particularly one with an $80 thousand grant?

2.  Identify problems that arise when community education classes are offered free to community participants.

3.  Discuss the role of volunteers in community education programs, and list the pros and cons of using volunteers.

4.  What future problems did Van Fone build into his program by paying extra-large salaries to his teaching staff?

5.  Describe some of Van Fone's early activities, and explain how they contributed to the community's immediate acceptance of community education.

6.  Discuss problems of too much money in relation to peer acceptance, salary structure, office equipment facilities, color TV, etc.

7.  Why did Van Fone's program fall off in attendance and enthusiasm in the second year? What effect did the grant have on the program?

8.  Describe Van Fone's meeting with the superintendent at the close of the case. Why had the superintendent called the meeting? When should this meeting have actually occurred?

## ACTIVITIES

1.  Develop a sample community education budget for three schools using the $80 thousand Van Fone was awarded.

2.  Rewrite a sample budget to project balanced funding from federal subsidies, local school resources, and industrial contributions. Include potential expansion into more facilities, assuming additional schools are available.

3.  Make a list of in-kind contributions that a school board might provide for matching funds for federal grants.

4. Develop the list of goals, strategies, and possibilities for funding and growth referred to in the case.

5. Role play the meeting between Dr. Matlock and Van Fone in an attempt to resolve Van Fone's funding problem.

CASE #18

## TO PAY OR NOT TO PAY

The regional meeting for community education directors began promptly at nine a.m., despite the fact that a few participants, preoccupied with renewing acquaintances, wandered around the room shaking hands and slapping backs. While the guest speaker was introduced, a small group of people hovered over the coffee urn, waiting to refill their cups.

There were over one hundred community education devotees in attendance. Comprising the cadre were not only community education directors but also state education department officials, university professors, superintendents, and board members.

A film culminated the speaker's presentation. As usual it was received warmly by those in attendance, many of whom had seen it once or twice before. About eleven a.m., a panel discussion was initiated. A few project reports were given; and key community education concepts were introduced, expanded, and embellished. The morning passed swiftly.

Jake Tanner, a part-time community education director for the Checkert Independent School District, ate very little of the buffet style lunch sponsored by the Templeton State Community Education Center. It was not because the food was bad or his stomach full. Engrossed in thought, he let his usual appetite elude him.

Tanner was in his first year of community education. He was also in his sixth year of teaching history at the high school. It had taken him six months to organize the project single-handedly. His first series of courses had been offered in the spring semester. Initially, all of his courses were filled to capacity. Later, attendance had fallen remarkably. The sudden decline in his enrollments he had largely attributed to an early spring. Although he had not ruled out the possibility that his courses were failing to meet the original expectations of participants, he was inclined to give the notion little thought. What bothered him most were the inconsistencies in his attendance ledger. Students dropped in and out of classes capriciously as if nothing of consequence ever transpired in between. It bothered his instructors even more. Their project esprit de corps was slowly disintegrating.

Tanner could find no fault in the project itself. The board of education and superintendent were firmly committed to it. He was running a variety of courses, fifteen to be exact. His instructors were specialists in the fields they taught. Participants paid nothing to attend the course or courses of their choice.

During the afternoon problem-solving session, Tanner kept quiet until Lew McCallum mentioned that he was having a bit of an attendance problem lately. "So am I," sparked Tanner, coming to life. "It's the early spring we're having." Tanner's eyes traveled over the faces of his colleagues.

"Anybody else having a problem?" asked McCallum.

"I've noted more absenteeism than usual," volunteered Bernie Tibbetts. "But the difference is negligible."

"I've lost half my enrollments, lost and gained them," Tanner said cryptically. "I mean," said Tanner, "that not only has my attendance shown a rapid decline, but also different people keep dropping in and out of class over extended periods of time." He shook his head. "I can't possibly imagine how they expect to benefit from the instruction." Pausing, he added, "My faculty is pretty upset about the matter." His expression turned morose.

"What kinds of courses are you offering?" asked Pat Arden.

"Those that the survey indicated the community was strongly in favor of," said Tanner smugly.

"Maybe it's your faculty!" suggested George Wilson. "I've had that problem. Almost ruined my program."

"George — It is George, isn't it?" asked Tanner. Wilson nodded, while Tanner continued to speak. "I've got a fine faculty, a devoted administration and board, and a building that never seems to put its lights out. I even offer the courses free to the community." Tanner folded his arms defensively.

"That could be your problem . . ." said McCallum, before he was interrupted by Tanner.

"What's that?" blinked Tanner.

"The fact that your patrons don't have to pay to attend," resumed McCallum. "Don't you see?" McCallum smiled. "There's no sense of commitment."

"To reverse an old adage," blurted out Wayne Stoffer, "the best things in life are not free, or at least, so we've been led to believe."

"That's true," said McCallum. "Value is often associated with cost. And when people pay, they want their money's worth. Moreover, there's a certain pride that comes from paying your own way."

"I agree," said Tibbetts, sliding forward in his chair. "Yet I might also add that when participants know it costs "x" number of dollars to run a course they identify as valuable, they have a tendency to become not only clients but also salesmen." Tibbetts moved to the edge of his seat. "And the more effort people put into a course to make it go, the more likely they are to be around when it finishes. A sense of commitment is the best kind of attendance stabilizer." Tibbets' eyes sparkled.

Tanner squirmed in his chair. "I think you boys are forgetting that in my project everyone has a chance to enroll. Not merely those who have money." Tanner looked indignant.

"But Jake," shouted Tibbetts, triumphantly, "you, yourself, implied that your patrons were lacking in commitment."

"There's another advantage in charging that we've been overlooking," Arden volunteered. "By charging we can offer a greater number and selection of courses. The wrong ones cancel themselves out; the right ones carry. Patrons are happier and the budget is balanced. Besides, the fee we charge is really only a pittance."

"If I may be so crude," laughed Stoffer, "when they pay, they stay." Everybody laughed, including Tanner.

Tanner stared at the ceiling for a moment, glassy eyed. Then, once again facing the group, he said uneasily, "OK, fellows, you've got me convinced. But how do I start putting a price tag on my courses without creating a furor in the community. The last thing I want to do is alienate anyone. Up to now we've been bragging about the fact that we take nothing but their time and try to give them everything they want." Tanner sighed, waiting for the group to reply.

## QUESTIONS

1. How effective is Tanner as a part-time administrator of a community education project?

2. Explain whether Tanner is justified in attributing declining class enrollments to an early spring.

3. What kind of attendance problem is Tanner having in his community education classes? How has this problem affected his instructors?

4. Discuss Tanner's philosophy of offering free courses. List the advantages and disadvantages of fee and free courses.

5. Compare Wayne Stoffer's philosophy with Jake Tanner's. Whose philosophy is more realistic?

6. How do McCallum and Tibbetts contribute to the development of Stoffer's philosophy?

7. React to Tanner's statement, "Everyone has a chance to enroll, not merely those who have money."

8. In what way does Tanner's philosophy place rigid restrictions on program development?

9. How can Tanner "start putting a price tag on courses without creating a furor in the community?"

10. Since Tanner has not done an evaluation of his program, how can he be sure that an absence of fees is his real problem?

## ACTIVITIES

1. Divide the class into two groups; fee vs. free. Build a rationale to support each philosophy.

2. Develop a budget form to be used to set up a community education program. Include staff salaries, secretarial help, supplies, maintenance, etc.

3. Poll the class to determine whether students support fee or free classes.

4. Develop two budget forms, each with a $12 thousand board investment. The first budget should reflect Tanner's current operation; the second, McCallum's.

5. Develop a fee structure that would support total program costs.

6. Develop a fee structure that would support only operating costs. Administrative costs are excluded.

7. Role play Tanner explaining to a class that future participation in community education will require a small fee.

## ANNOTATED READINGS

Berridge, Robert I. *The Community Education Handbook*, Midland, Michigan: Pendell Publishing Company, 1973. Chapter IV, Financing. One of the first questions asked when project implementation is being considered is how the project will be financed; a second is how it will be budgeted. This chapter describes line item entries for a typical project budget and shows a method of ascertaining programming costs. The reader is provided a sample budget outline and two budgets, one for a small community and one for a large community.

Chopia, Ray. "Money — Who Needs It?", *Community Education Journal*, Volume IV, No. 5, Sept./Oct. 1974, (pp. 51-52). The main thrust of the article is how to build a unified community education program without additional costs to local school districts. The answer is in the level of involvement of available human and physical resources and in the incorporation of these resources into a total community education program.

Doherty, David J. "Education and Industry: Will They Help One Another Survive?", *Community Education Journal*, Volume II, No. 3, May 1972, (pp. 35-38). Cooperation with industry is imperative to the development of an educational system in a community. The author contends that the community education director should make every effort to cooperate with businessmen. A list of suggestions to attain the desired relationship is offered to the reader.

Hickey, Howard W., and Van Voorhees, Curtis. *The Role of the School in Community Education*, Midland, Michigan: Pendell Publishing Company, 1969. Chapter VIII, Community School: Financing, written by Raymond L. Boozer. A philosophical approach to funding and various sources of funds are discussed in the chapter. The process of determining a workable budget in the light of cost factors is also examined.

Minzey, Jack, and LeTarte, Clyde E. *From Program to Process*, Midland, Michigan: Pendell Publishing Company, 1972, (pp. 203-225). Minzey and LeTarte lead the reader into looking at the cost factors of a new community education program and then go on to list in detail sixteen sources for securing funds for community education programs. The latter part of the section is devoted to an analysis of the components of a community education budget. Sample budgetary forms are included.

Pappadakas, Nick. "Financing Community Education," *Community Education Journal*, Volume I, No. 2, May 1971, (pp. 37-41, 59). The article is divided into major sections, such as the need for financing, priorities, sources available nationally, state financing, and other sources of funding. Though some of the funding sources given in the article are out-of-date, the article does offer an overall picture of the funding procedure.

Pappadakas, Nick, and Totten, Fred W. "Financing the New Dimensions of Community Education," *Phi Delta Kappan*, Volume LIV, No. 3, November 1972, (pp. 192-194). The authors review the financing of community education from many perspectives. Initially discussed is the boot strap financing pattern that has evolved in many communities. The six to eight percent cost of community education listed by the authors includes some costs which may already be borne by a school district; thus they are not added costs of community education. A list of funding sources is included in the article.

Parson, Steve R. "Who Is Going to Pay the Bills?", *Community Education Journal,* Volume V, No. 1, February 1975, (p. 41). Parson deals with the reality of community education — that it does cost money and that alternative funding methods are needed to assist local school districts. Examples of how some states and local school districts have come up with funding programs are provided. The new idea of federal revenue sharing is also highlighted in this article.

Ramsey, Russell A. "A Community School — Without Special Funding," *Community Education Journal,* Volume IV, No. 1, Jan./Feb. 1974 (pp. 30-32). This article focuses upon a school district that initiated community education without special program funding. The key was the involvement of outside organizations and agencies to pick up the programming, with the school district using some unique methods of sharing the salary of the coordinator.

Whitt, Robert L. *A Handbook for the Community School Director,* Midland, Michigan: Pendell Publishing Company, 1971. Chapter VII, The Community School Director and Fiscal Responsibility. The author states that there should be a much broader definition of school finance, one that would include monies for the social reconstruction of society. From this philosophical base the chapter moves into the development of a budget for a community education project and into procedures for administering the budget. The chapter contains a list of eleven specific administrative procedures.

# CHAPTER 7 Exercising Leadership

The success of a community education project is directly proportional to the leadership skills of the individual responsible for the project's implementation and dissemination. Success is, therefore, contingent upon the individual who is personally and professionally qualified to lead both school and community.

Leadership is not simply a matter of rank; in its ideal sense it is an honor earned. And as such, leadership epitomizes the democratic style so essential for cooperative planning and programming in community education. Opportunities to share in the decision-making process must be afforded all who participate under the auspices of the community education umbrella. Through the development of broad participatory frameworks, the community education director is able to involve every segment of the community in new and more meaningful levels of decision-making. With a consensus of opinion, he acts with indisputable credentials. The director must be prepared, however, to make and enforce final policy decisions whenever necessary to extend and embellish the life of community education in his or her community.

The leader of the community education program must have compassion and understanding when dealing with cross-sections of the community. He or she must appreciate the value of individual differences, yet be aware of the importance these differences might have on the total organization of the project. Finally, the director must be in good emotional and physical health and full of enthusiasm and vigor.

It would seem that the leadership skills and personal attributes needed for a successful community education director verge on the extraordinary. Nevertheless, the complex responsibilities of the director virtually demand a herculean effort. Unfortunately, school systems, too often, employ part-time directors to implement their community education projects. What results is a job poorly done.

Though the concept of leadership can be broached with varying degrees of success in any of the preceding cases, leadership becomes in this chapter a study in itself. Here skills, attributes, and styles of actual or assumed leaders are brought together for an extended analysis. Here, too, agencies and institutions vie for leadership roles, driven by the persons who lead them.

Who should initiate and implement community education in the community is the question which arises in the first case. Should the director of parks and recreation, for example, assume the leadership role in a community education project, or should leadership be shared by agency and school alike?

In the second case the role of the community college in community education is examined. As more and more community colleges are built in local communities, the quest for community college leadership in community education grows in intensity. Since institutional leadership cannot be divorced from human capabilities, the problem of who can and will lead once again arises.

Leadership styles become the center of attraction in the last case, where a superintendent must choose between two directors to fill the position of coordinator. Although both men appear to perform adequately in their present positions, each has a different leadership style. The crux of the problem is to determine which leadership style is better for administering a city-wide program. Perhaps the answer is neither!

CASE #19

## FOLLOW THE LEADER

At fifty, Tony Bailey, the director of the Dalesboro Parks and Recreation Department discovered community education. Having worked with youth and school officials all his life, he was fully aware of what the full utilization of schools could mean to both young and old alike. When he shared his idea with his superior, he was encouraged to move ahead in his plans. Two weeks later, Bailey, outspoken and muscular, with pitch black hair and twinkling blue eyes, seemed to tower far above his average height when he enthusiastically addressed the Dalesboro Board of Education. With rapt attention, the board listened to his plan.

Bailey spoke of extended programs for youth, new programs for the very young and old, and multiple course offerings for parents desiring to further educational needs or broaden recreational interests. He also spoke of coordinated efforts in the scheduling of educational facilities and community resources to eliminate program redundancies. When he finished his presentation, the board applauded his ebullience and initiative. A couple of board members seriously wondered why the administration, namely their superintendent, wasn't providing the school district with this kind of leadership, but most were simply grateful that Bailey was willing to do the job at no expense to the district. Their main concern was to provide their constituents with as many benefits as possible from each tax dollar. How this was accomplished did not really matter.

Before leaving the board room, Bailey vigorously shook the hand of every board member. All were flattered that he knew their names, most of them having met him only tonight. But Bailey was a stickler for names and faces; and casual contacts and newspaper photographs served his memory well.

Bailey was slightly dismayed as he shook the hand of Superintendent Kayle. Their brief interlocking of hands conveyed to him an attitude of indifference, perhaps, even envy. His victory, however, quickly blocked the thought out of his mind. Later that night he was to experience a sense of irritation. It was a feeling of having overlooked something or, worse yet, erred, which he could neither explain nor relate to his previous activities. Since everything was going his way, he eventually dismissed it.

Bailey and his two assistants, Doug Tinzer and Mel Jacobs, implemented their full-utilization concept three months after Bailey's presentation to the board. In between, they had attended a two week training session in community education, established a community advisory council, conducted a survey, and identified three schools, a high school, a middle school, and an elementary school, as project sites. Additional project sites would be chosen later.

Bailey's first difficulty arose when he began hiring noncertificated personnel to teach his courses. The teachers in Dalesboro did not like to be deprived of extra income. Bailey was mainly interested in amassing volunteers and in employing his parks and recreation people. However, to pacify the disgruntled teachers, Bailey modified his hiring practices. His new goal was a fifty-fifty split, half Dalesboro teachers and half his own cadre.

The interviews he conducted with teachers led him into further problems. His selection process chagrined the teaching staff. It was their feeling that if they applied they should be hired. To them, there were none more capable than they for the task at hand. Bailey disagreed emphatically.

Meanwhile, the principals in each of the three schools continued to schedule activities as they had been doing for years. The communications gap between parks and recreation and the Dalesboro administrators widened during the period of program implementation as scheduling conflicts multiplied.

Eventually, the custodial force lodged a series of complaints about unusually dirty classrooms, littered corridors, and abused facilities and grounds. The teachers followed up the complaints by filing a formal grievance over missing personal belongings and damaged school property. Ultimately, the principals quarreled with the parks and recreation people and virtually demanded that they leave the school premises. Amidst it all, the superintendent sat back and waited, feeling only estrangement for the program.

When it became absolutely necessary that the issue be resolved by the members of the board, Bailey placed the matter in their hands. He attended the board meeting accompanied by his two assistants and at least fifty of the local citizenry. Though the superintendent came alone, many of his principals and teachers were present at the meeting.

Bailey, not his ordinary self, looked disheveled and bleary-eyed. His face was gaunt and his posture defensive. Months of hard work and sleepless nights were written on his furrowed brow.

During the proceedings, he attributed the failure of the program to the superintendent.

"He gave me no help whatsoever!" growled Bailey. "He could have straightened out the whole mess any time he felt like it. But he didn't, as we all know only too well."

Superintendent Kayle wore the expression of a slighted friend when he quietly but eloquently responded to the indictment.

"Mr. Bailey, did you ever seek my help? Did you once pick up the phone to call me? Have you ever dropped by my office for a chat? I think not. You wanted to provided sole leadership for this program, yet you presented it to us not too many months ago as a collaborative effort." Kayle paused. "Let me assure you, Mr. Bailey, that whenever you are ready to work with me, I shall be most willing to work with you."

Bailey was abashed. He frantically searched the faces of the audience, his assistants, the board, and then looked again in bewilderment at the superintendent. The answer was not to be seen in their faces. It would have to come from him. Suddenly his face broke into an understanding smile. He knew what he had to say, what he should have said a long time ago, what had troubled him since the beginning. Already, he could see the superintendent returning his smile. In a moment the future of community education in Dalesboro would be secure.

## QUESTIONS

1. Why does Superintendent Kayle appear to be disinterested in community education? How might Bailey have involved Kayle in his project? What benefits would Bailey have derived from collaborating with Kayle?

2. What actions should Bailey have taken to gain the support of the Dalesboro teachers?

3. What is wrong with Bailey's quota system — "fifty-fifty split, half Dalesboro teachers and half his own cadre?"

4. How might Bailey have avoided the conflicts which developed between his people and school personnel?

5. What mistake in public relations did Bailey make when he initiated the community education project?

6. What other institutions and agencies in the community besides the school might Bailey have alienated by his planning?

7. Why did Bailey seek an open board meeting to resolve his problems? What other methods might he have employed?

8. Should the leadership for community education come from outside the public school domain? If so, support your answer by citing examples of successful projects.

## ACTIVITIES

1. List the advantages and disadvantages of having a community education project initiated by an organization other than the public school.

2. Role play a meeting between Bailey and associates and three building principals to improve working relationships.

3. List additional organizations and agencies that might be able to implement community education in a community and develop a rationale to assess their likelihood to succeed.

4. Role play Bailey responding to the superintendent's offer to collaborate with him on the community education project.

5. Poll the class to determine whether the school should be the sole proprietor of community education.

CASE #20

## A CONFLICT OF INTERESTS

It was three in the afternoon when Phil Tompkins entered the Forestbrook Community College Administration Building. Actually he had first set foot on the campus about two hours earlier. Since he was a newcomer to Charlotte City, he wanted to acquaint himself with the layout of the campus before he met with the community college president and the continuing education director. It was not his intention to impress his reluctant hosts with a knowledge of their instructional capabilities; it was strictly business — more precisely, community education business! Tompkins, an out-of-stater, had come to Charlotte City in March to initiate and operationalize a community education program in the public school system by the subsequent fall. That was three weeks ago.

Since his arrival Tompkins had gained the unanimous support of the Citizens for a Better Community, a task which had been relatively simple, considering that at least 80 percent of the organization had been primarily responsible for his employment. He had also enlisted the aid of several service clubs, the city's churchfathers, prominent industrialists and businessmen, and the parks and recreation people. He had not, however, made much headway with the director of the continuing education program at Forestbrook Community College whose voice had vociferously delivered the only nay in the crowd assembled in the civic auditorium a week before when an open vote of confidence was taken. The reason for Tompkin's visit to Forestbrook was, therefore, elementary. He meant to win over to his side the president of the community college and, in doing so, reverse the official position of his subordinate.

Dr. Paul Scott, Forestbrook's president for the past five years, rose to welcome Tompkins when he stepped into his office. His handshake was firm and friendly, and his face was all smile. The continuing education director, on the other hand, dispatched his amenities with shades of indifference and hostility.

In the center of the large room, overlooking a vinyl-covered divan and two stout upholstered chairs, was a prodigious mahogany desk partially covered by a plate of thick glass. To the right of the desk was a long rectangular table, surrounded by padded, straight wooden chairs. It was to this heavily polished table that Tompkins was led, his feet sinking into plush carpeting.

When the three men seated themselves, Dr. Scott positioned himself at the head of the dark table, with his associate on his right and Tompkins on his left. The president cheerfully opened the conversation.

"Jack has been telling me about some of the plans you have for implementing community education in our fair city. He says you envision your school district as some kind of catalyst that will prompt us into better servicing the needs of our community."

Jack Starr stared out the window, stifling a yawn.

Brushing away a wisp of grayish blond hair that had fallen across his forehead, President Scott, in a pose that highlighted his classical features, continued his monologue. There was a slight trace of sarcasm in his voice, which Tompkins could not help detecting.

"Ordinarily, I let Jack run his own show. In fact, had you not insisted upon this meeting, we might never have met. Since you are here — and by the way, I admire your perseverance — why don't you tell me what *you have in mind!*" President Scott leaned back comfortably in his chair.

Tompkins crossed his legs and nervously scratched his knee.

"First of all, let me assure you that while the community school may precipitate the community education movement, it does not necessarily follow that we see ourselves as exercising sole leadership. It is, instead, our idea to share the leadership function through a series of cooperative efforts aimed at the elimination of program redundancies and at the creation of innovative program opportunities. If your institution is better equipped to provide a service than any of the other participating agencies or organizations, the task is ostensibly yours." Tompkins waited for a reaction. What he received was a nod which encouraged him to go on.

"As you well know, most of us, however well-meaning, have a tendency to replicate our efforts when we attempt to do our thing in isolation from others, also well-meaning, who are doing pretty much the same thing. What I want to accomplish with your help is the development of a clear-cut organizational plan that will link all community efforts together. And with the proper communication networks, we can do exactly that."

Jack Starr suddenly came alive. His eyes widened and his breathing was conspicuous.

"Look here, Tompkins," gasped Starr, beginning to fume. "Why don't you admit that we can do the job better than anybody else, and let it go at that. You'll start by initiating a flock of programs, then quadruple them. Before long, I suspect, you'll be the one who's spinning the community's wheels. We don't need any more programs in this community; and what we do need Forestbrook can handle more than adequately without your help. I suggest you take the time to explore our facility." Starr's shoulders drooped as he relaxed.

Responding with mild confidence, Tompkins said, "I have explored your facility. Prior to my coming to this office, I did a lot of investigating."

"All right," said Starr, surprised, "then you've noticed that it's new, huge, and growing fast. We have educational television plugged into our classrooms and community cable networks that reach the home with a variety of our programs. We offer an open door policy, nontraditional education, academic education, vocational and avocational education, and recreation programs. We have individualization of instruction and a gigantic library. Furthermore, we have noncredit and credit course structures; and our fees are exceedingly reasonable. What more can a community ask for? From us they get status. What do they get from you?" Starr's upper lip curled as he finished his statement.

"They get from us a sense of community in an age of isolationism and alienation," answered Tompkins quietly. "They get involved in the democratic process, not just participate in ready-made programs. They have opportunities to plan their own needs as a group of interested citizens, choosing their own courses through block surveys which occur at the smallest unit of self-governance. They also get accustomed to school again before they venture on to larger campuses, such as yours."

"The way you keep rambling on," said Starr caustically, "our leadership role diminishes by the second."

"Hold on, Jack," interrupted President Scott. "Perhaps we're being a trifle unfair. I'd like to hear the rest of the community education story. I find it very interesting."

"I admit," said Tompkins, unfolding his arms, "that Forestbrook would outshine us by far in any instructional endeavor that we might attempt within the confines of our public school classrooms. You have sophisticated teaching expertise and expansive and well-equipped buildings that contain the latest in instructional technology. But we, in conjunction with the other agencies that share our belief, see ourselves as basically grassroots. We tackle problems, large and small, at the neighborhood level, such as acquiring street lamps to make a darkly lit and dangerous street safer for residents, getting improved sewage facilities for neighborhoods that need them, organizing clean-up campaigns for run-down segments of the community, helping a troubled youth, a senior citizen, feeding a hungry child, who must eat to learn. . . . I could go on indefinitely. All I ask is that you join us, not compete with us."

President Scott stiffened in his chair as a heavy silence pervaded the room. With raised eyebrows, he said, thoughtfully, "Before I give you my decision, which I won't deny is at this moment positive, I must make one very legitimate request."

"Ask on," blurted Tompkins, excitedly.

"Please define what you conceive to be Forestbrook's role in the community endeavor."

Tompkins reached into his briefcase and quickly withdrew a looseleaf folder of bulging proportions.

"I am only too happy to share my ideas with you, provided, of course, that you are willing to share with me and others the leadership prerogative that we have been discussing. Stop me, whenever you wish."

Starr laughed raucously. "Don't worry. We will!"

When President Scott frowned at his associate, Tompkins put his left hand under the table and crossed his fingers tightly. In his other hand, he held the plan he would soon be describing.

## QUESTIONS

1. What should be the role of the community college in community education and how should it differ from the role of other agencies and organizations in a community?

2. Who should exercise primary leadership in a community education project? Is there any advantage in having a community college president serve as project leader?

3. Why did Starr oppose the community education movement? What did Tompkins do to combat his negativism, and how successful was he in his endeavor?

4. What would Tompkins have accomplished by meeting with Starr before he met with the community college president?

5. Why should a community college feel threatened by a community education project?

6. Compare continuing education and adult education. What are the primary differences?

7. How might a community education project be beneficial to a community college? Identify areas of interest shared by the community school and the community college, and develop coopera-

tive strategies among institutions, agencies, and organizations which would enhance the community education movement.

## ACTIVITIES

1.  List some overlap and duplication of services commonly present in a community with both a community college and a community education program.

2.  Brainstorm ways in which the community college could work synergistically with a community education project.

3.  What are the immediate and long-range academic benefits that a community college might derive from operating in a community education project?

4.  Compare the funding pattern of community colleges with community schools, and explain why community education could pose a financial threat to the community college.

5.  Review current journal articles that discuss the role of community colleges in community education, and report to the class your findings.

6.  Outline Tompkins' plan for cooperating with the community college in his upcoming community project.

CASE #21

# THE NEW COORDINATOR

The Traymont School District was on the verge of beginning its third year of community education when its project coordinator resigned to accept an administrative post in another school system. Carl Tucker, Traymont's superintendent of schools, bore no ill-feelings toward the capable administrator he was losing, despite his August first resignation. Tucker had always advocated professional advancement. The coordinator had served the district well and, therefore, deserved every opportunity to improve himself professionally. Had Tucker been able to duplicate or exceed the benefits that his subordinate would derive from his new position, he would have most certainly done so. As it was, he bade the coordinator goodbye, wishing him the best of success.

To the dismay of the two directors, who were both vying for their superordinate's vacated position, Tucker looked outside of the district for a possible replacement. Though he did not encourage the community education directors to apply, neither did he discourage them from submitting their applications. He merely made it evident to them at the outset of the search that they would probably be competing with a substantial number of other candidates.

Having contacted some fifty placement centers across the country, Tucker shortly began receiving letters of application and placement papers from a variety of job seekers. Unfortunately, the qualifications of all of the candidates fell considerably short of meeting his expectations for the position. It was Tucker's conclusion that the lateness of the year was responsible for the lack of the best-qualified candidates.

Eventually, Tucker surmised that it would be easier to promote one of his directors to the position of coordinator and hire a new director than it would be to find the coordinator he had in mind. At least, reasoned Tucker, his directors were running their programs successfully, and to that extent they had proved themselves. Moreover, they knew the district well, its schools, programs, and people. Tucker had to admit that even an experienced newcomer would not have that advantage; and an inexperienced one would be doubly disadvantaged. As each day passed, he kept hoping that he would discover the applicant of his choice. But the day never came. Meanwhile, his procrastination threatened to jeopardize the community education project.

Nine days before school started, Tucker finally decided to choose one of his directors for the position. Once that was done, he and his coordinator would pick a new director. Then everything would be normal again.

Tucker came to his office early Monday morning with a headache. He had spent the entire weekend thinking about the professional and personal qualifications of his directors. Three sleepless nights had been the result. After two cups of coffee and a pipeful of tobacco, Tucker carefully recounted his thoughts.

Barry Smith, the director of the program at the high school, was reputed to be extremely autocratic. He was not well-liked by the members of his staff, but he was definitely respected. While they did not go out of their way to help him, none dared to oppose him. Tucker, himself, did not enjoy the man's company; for some strange reason, which he could not explain, he usually felt inferior in his presence.

Smith went by the book and was a stickler for rules. He was aggressive, confident, ambitious, and fairly intelligent. He was unquestionably a responsible person and always got things done on time. There was no significant program growth to be attributed to his leadership, for he was primarily a maintainer rather than an initiator. But, on the other hand, his program had never regressed an iota. He strongly believed in community education and was thoroughly acquainted with its precepts and programs.

Thirty-six years old, the father of five children, and apparently happily married, Smith was not only a native of the community but also an active participant in community affairs. Smith, a teacher at twenty-two, had spent eleven years in the classroom teaching biology and three in community education directing a community school. His highest degree was a Master of Science in education with a major in educational administration. In addition, he had amassed another thirty credits while working toward a superintendency credential.

The other director, a former community education fellow and the recipient of a master's degree in educational administration, was Terrence McDonald. With no ostensible difficulty, McDonald ran a community education program in the newest and largest elementary school in the district. His course offerings were extensive, and his enrollments enormous. Staff and students spoke highly of him. On one occasion they had surprised him with a birthday party, on another with an anniversary party commemorating his twenty-fifth year of marriage. Superintendent Tucker often received letters praising McDonald beyond belief.

But Tucker was, as well, the receiver of many complaints about

McDonald. The custodian told Tucker that the school was becoming impossible to clean because of McDonald. Several of the regular teaching staff, forming an ad hoc group, had personally addressed Tucker to demand that McDonald be admonished for his laxity in the building. Added to these complaints were those of the business manager who considered McDonald's accounting methods positively bizzare. "He would lose his shirt," he told Tucker over lunch one day, "if his wife didn't button it on him." A few times during the onset of the program, a few members of his staff had even complained. They were concerned about his never being available for assistance. Later, after they had learned that it was up to them to fend for themselves, they became accustomed to having their own way and were openly thankful for the opportunity to do their own thing.

It was not that McDonald was stupid. Actually, he was exceptionally intelligent. His academic record and aptitude test attested to this fact. Furthermore, it was not that he wished to avoid responsibility; he merely wanted to share it. He constantly preached participative management, whenever he could find an audience.

Many of the regular staff believed him to be intentionally careless. Others more knowledgeable about the range of his activities said that he was over-extending himself by becoming involved in too many neighborhood projects. Almost everyone admired him for his overwhelming interest in people, but a few found his inefficiency intolerable.

In his home McDonald was also said to be easy-going, the effect of which was quite obvious. He had two fine children, now grown up, who were independent, intelligent, industrious, and affable, and a loving wife to whom he had been married for twenty-six years. Though both his children had graduated from college, married, and moved away, they visited him often. McDonald's neighbor, and personal friend of Tucker's wife, had frequently extolled his virtues to the superintendent's wife. Once she stated to Mrs. Tucker, "Terry McDonald is one of the finest persons I have ever met. He thinks the world of people and can't do enough to help them."

In summing up his thoughts, Superintendent Tucker conjectured that under McDonald's direction the program would either grow in leaps and bounds or someday collapse entirely. Of Barry Smith's kind of leadership, he could be sure. As long as Smith was around, the program would be ongoing. But would it grow, he asked himself. While he continued to think about the strengths and weaknesses of the two directors, his eyes traveled over to the shelf where the placement folders of the applicants were perched. Maybe he was being too hasty in his decision about not hiring a person with less experience than his directors.

When his phone buzzed and his secretary reminded him of his ten o'clock meeting with the administrative staff, he was still trying to make a decision.

## QUESTIONS

1. Define the difference between a coordinator and a community school director as distinguished in this case.

2. To promote from within or hire from outside the district is a constant problem facing public school superintendents. In the area of community education, which method of hiring is better? Support your answer.

3. Is there any reason to believe that a good community school director would not make an effective central office coordinator? Explain.

4. In view of the fact that the Traymont School District had only two buildings involved in community education, did the project actually require the leadership of a coordinator? Who might have handled this leadership role?

5. Discuss the pros and cons of bringing in an outside person to coordinate Traymont's community education program.

6. Identify strengths and weaknesses in each of the two community school directors. If you were Superintendent Tucker, whom would you have chosen for the position, and why?

## ACTIVITIES

1. List the technical, human and conceptual skills needed by the community school director and community education coordinator.

2. Identify the leadership styles of both directors and discuss the appropriateness of these styles for the role of community school director.

3. Role play a position interview with Tucker and each of the two community school directors.

4. What is the difference between a leader and an administrator? Define what is meant by leadership. Discuss various leadership styles in terms of their implications for advancing community education. What leadership style is best for community educators?

5. Compare and contrast the position descriptions of coordinators and community school directors in three different school districts.

## ANNOTATED READINGS

Bell, Ted, "Key Chain of Leadership," *Community Education Journal*, Volume II, No. 4, (pp. 24-26). The successful initiation of community education projects involves leadership at the national, state, and local levels. In discussing the leadership role of the state department, the author provides examples of leadership activities in several states.

Burden, Larry, and Whitt, Robert L. *The Community School Principal*, Midland, Michigan: Pendell Publishing Company, 1973, (pp. 3-36). A comprehensive look at leadership, as it reflects the role of the community school principal is focused on in this section. Definitions, styles, models, theories, and theoreticians receive varying degrees of consideration. Management function grids, technical skills dealing with staff, decision-making processes, and a series of case studies are considered, as well.

DeLargy, Paul F. "Training Essential to Achieve Community Education Goals," *Community Education Journal*, Volume V, No. 3, May/June 1975, (p. 33). The author discusses eighteen goal areas in community education that specify that training is needed to insure successful implementation of community education programs. These skills must be part of the leadership training package made available to the professional community educator. To omit or disregard the impact of these goal areas is to deny the full potential of a comprehensive program.

Kerensky, V. M., and Melby, Ernest O. *Education II — The Social Imperative*, Midland, Michigan: Pendell Publishing Company, 1971, (pp. 137-140). The authors use ten characteristics to develop a profile of an educational leader. Following the profile is a brief discussion of McGregor's theory. The authors conclude with a look at the newly emerging education and its implications for key leadership.

Nance, Everette E. "Training the Bosses," *Community Education Journal*, Volume V, No. 3, May/June 1975, (p. 47). Nance, excluding the public school sector, focuses upon the high level leadership in community education. He relates training needs to four areas and discusses their functions, role, and training as representative leadership components in successful support of community education.

Nance, Everette E. "The University's Role in Training the Community Educator," *Community Education Journal*, Volume V, No. 1, Jan./Feb. 1975, (p. 31). The author discusses eight major training areas for leadership personnel in community education. Also discussed are five areas of the training component needed for successful leadership skills. Finally, some thoughts on the certification of people in leadership roles of community education are included. A challenge is issued to universities on their readiness to handle the training role of the new leadership required for community education.

Seay, Maurice F., and Associates. *Community Education: A Developing Concept*, Midland, Michigan: Pendell Publishing Company, 1974, (pp. 85-144;

329-347). Two complete chapters dealing with leadership are highlighted in Seay's text. Boles and Weaver present two differing dimensions of leadership. One focuses on theory; the other on practice as it pertains to training the community educator. Charts, illustrations and models are included in the two chapters. Another chapter deals with "The Role of the Community College in Community Education."

Sullivan, Edward A. "The Community School Principal," *Community Education Journal*, Volume II, No. 3, May 1972, (pp. 29-30). The article asks and answers the questions: What type of preparation should the community school principal undergo? What should his relationship be to the community school director? What should his role be, if any, in the community school program? How can he relate the K-12 program to the after-school and evening programs? It is suggested that the preparation program for the community school principal should involve the following: teaching experience, graduate work of an interdisciplinary nature, simulation training, and internship.

Totten, Fred. *The Power of Community Education*, Midland, Michigan: Pendell Publishing Company, 1970, (pp. 19, 128, 157). The author refers to leadership as the primary ingredient needed for successful community education programming. He states that leadership in community education comes from many quarters. It may come from youth, adults, and senior citizens. Examples and illustrations are cited to give the reader some insight into how this leadership is developed.

Winecoff, Larry, and Powell, Conrad. "Volunteer and Paraprofessional Training," *Community Education Journal*, Volume V, No. 3, May/June 1975, (pp. 48-55). The authors provide an in-depth look at volunteers and paraprofessionals as a second line support of leadership in successful community education administration and programming. A comprehensive look into the training of these two vital support systems to community education is offered.

# Evaluating Programs and Projects

## CHAPTER 8

Since the rise of community education to levels of national and international awareness, critics have increasingly demanded that community educators become more accountable. Unfortunately, the hows and whys and even whens of evaluation are questions which remain largely unanswered by those closely associated with the community education movement. Everyone agrees that something needs to be done, but no one seems to know precisely what that something is. As a result, little progress has been made in the development of sophisticated research techniques.

Generally speaking, community education has gained awareness and intensity through the efforts of educators, whose orientation is toward people, not research. Indeed, one of the initiators and leaders of community education often stated that research would get in the way of helping people and that the movement would have never reached its present-day level if community educators had stopped to research every step they took.

There has been a strong feeling among leaders against the stereotyping or cookbooking of community education. Some still claim that community education cannot be defined. Others, very much immersed in activities which continue to extend the meaning and scope of community education, would prefer that definition become subordinate to growth. The fact is community education can be defined, planned, and evaluated, despite the unique and personalized contribution it makes to each community. Now that the accountability stage has been reached, community educators must act. The day of accepting claims based only on subjective data has apparently passed. This does not mean that community educators are turning away from the person in the program; merely that they wish to measure program effectiveness in serving that person in the best possible manner.

Although specific goals have been established in some community projects, these goals are often poorly conceived and written by a steering committee under the guidance of a community education coordinator who lacks research skills. Attempts at research and evaluation in ongoing community education programs have been frequently conducted under similar conditions.

It would appear that community educators can no longer overlook the need of having trained researchers in the field. One way to meet this need is to retrain an experienced community educator as a researcher. It seems more likely, however, that the future of community education holds a prominent place for both practitioner and researcher in community education projects, each complementing the other in a vibrant and viable partnership.

The three cases that follow have been written to involve the student in the problems of research and evaluation. In the first case a superintendent and a community education director are confronted by a university evaluation team that equates program success with the development of a list of short- and long-range goals. In the second case a coordinator is challenged by a group of university students for his dependence upon subjective data to validate project gains. What should be evaluated is the question posed in the final case — the value of one human life or the meeting of a myriad of abstract goals.

**CASE #22**

## EVALUATION DAY

Superintendent Ben Dayton buzzed his secretary in the small reception area adjoining his office.

"Yes, Mr. Dayton," the secretary's voice purred.

"Has Roy Mavis arrived yet?" he snapped impatiently.

"No, Mr. Dayton." The purr changed to a whine.

"Will you please check the switchboard, Ruth?" said Dayton more evenly. The whine had prodded him into regaining some of his composure. "Maybe, he left word with Mrs. Swain. I can't understand why he's so late." He sighed. "He's usually very prompt."

"I'll check, Mr. Dayton," she said, the purr returning to her voice.

Dayton lighted a cigar and puffed at it furiously. Soon huge gray clouds hovered over his head. There they lingered, seemingly suspended on the bright rays of sunlight which beamed through a double window.

When Roy Mavis popped into his office, the cigar was a stub in Dayton's hand. He mashed its remains as Mavis crumbled breathlessly into a chair to the right of him.

"Roy, what in heaven's name took you so long?" Dayton frowned. "I've been waiting for you over an hour," he said angrily.

"I had a few last minute imperatives to take care of before the university center evaluation team got here," said Mavis apologetically. "I'm really sorry. I know how concerned you are. But you'd be a lot more concerned if I had neglected my responsibilities." With his second breath came some of his usual confidence. The two men stared at each other momentarily.

"You're right," Dayton nodded. "Only you should have called," he said peevishly. "Well, how does everything look? Are we ready to exhibit seven years of community education to the university brass?" he said jocularly. "We should be pros at it by now. We've been entertaining visitors from school districts for years."

"Everything looks just fine," grinned Mavis. "In fact, it's days like today that make me want to go on being a community education director for the next one hundred years." The grin turned into a broad smile.

"You should live so long!" quipped Dayton, returning the other man's smile. Dayton perked up. "What's the agenda for the community education evaluators?" he asked cheerfully.

"To begin with, I've charted our program growth, showing how we started with a program next to nothing in one school and expanded it into twenty to thirty courses in seven schools," Mavis said proudly, inflating his chest somewhat conspicuously.

"Next, I've got a tour set up for the evaluators to observe our preschool program in action. While we're at it, I'm going to casually suggest a head count of the number of volunteers we've tied into our programs. That alone should earn us a gold star. My last count was sixty-two."

Engrossed in his delivery, Mavis rambled on exuberantly. He seemed to marvel at his numerous accomplishments. It was as if he were actually seeing, for the first time, the far flung results of his labors. The pictures danced in his head.

Dayton interrupted a monologue that was fast becoming a reverie. "You are going to arrange for the team to view our after-school electives program at the high school," he said in a questioning tone.

"By all means!" said Mavis happily, still intoxicated by his vision of success. "Not only will I have the evaluators see our program, but also I plan to have them interview students and staff about its overwhelming success. This can be done during the lunch periods."

Mavis yanked out a small notebook from his back pocket. Paling slightly, he mumbled, "Almost forgot." He flicked through the book's pages clumsily. "I've got to call Hank Grunwald from parks and recreation. He's the only one who hasn't given me a confirmation on this afternoon's meeting."

"How many agencies and organizations are going to be involved in the meeting?" asked the superintendent, unable to conceal his excitement.

"I've got the Y.M.C.A., the Y.W.C.A., the police and health departments, PTA's and PTO's, a representative from the mayor's office, two of our Golden Years volunteers, several service clubs, and, of course, parks and recreation as soon as I get hold of Hank Grunwald. I should have twenty people in all. On top of that," said Mavis, slapping his knee, "tonight is family night."

"Then we can expect an unusually large turnout," said the superintendent ecstatically.

"Rest assured." Mavis stood up. "I think I better try to contact Grunwald. I'm sure he'll be there, but I want to remind him, if necessary."

"Take it easy," said Dayton, getting up. "You're making me nervous. Henry hasn't forgotten a meeting yet." Dayton scratched the stubble under his chin, which suddenly annoyed him. With his heavy beard he was rarely able to get a clean shave, no matter how hard he tried.

"On the other hand," said Dayton, rubbing his chin until the skin became mildly irritated, "if it makes you feel better, call him right now. Here, you can use my phone." The superintendent left the room carrying an empty coffee cup.

At ten a.m. the university evaluating team from the regional community education center entered the office of the superintendent. On hand to greet them were Dayton and Mavis. After a series of introductions and a couple of rounds of handshaking, the five men seated themselves, each waiting for the other to speak.

Then Mavis broke the silence of the room with what seemed like an unending flow of figures, facts, programs, and finally the team's itinerary for the day, all of which seemed to be treated with indifference by the team.

Having finished his five-minute speech, Mavis waited deliriously for the team's congratulatory remarks. Instead of receiving the praise he thought due him, however, he was to witness a rapid number of brief exchanges — glances and whispers which lent an ominous quality to the atmosphere of the room.

Noting Mavis' dismay, the senior member of the team spoke up quickly and authoritatively.

"All of what you've been telling us is very fine," he said, vaguely reassuring. "Very fine, indeed. Nevertheless," he added in a rather critical tone of voice, "what we're really interested in seeing are your long-range goals or objectives. We want to examine your original plan. We want to see how you PERT out the activities in your flow chart, how far you've come in terms of accomplishing short-range goals, and how and when you plan to reach your major goals. With that kind of data, we can begin to evaluate your program. To put it bluntly, gentlemen, we don't want the cake; we want the recipe." His colleagues grunted in agreement.

The senior member of the team stared at the stunned faces of the school administrators. He could almost anticipate their reply. He had seen the look and heard similar replies before, time and time again.

The community education director cleared his throat to eliminate the hoarseness that accompanied his words.

"We don't have any goals. But we do have an excellent program. Anyone that has ever visited our schools will attest to that." Mavis was loudly defensive.

"Attest, yes," said the senior evaluator gravely, "but evaluate, no! Please keep in mind," he added pedantically, "if you don't know where you're going, how will you ever know when you've arrived!"

"So what do you recommend that we do?" asked the superintendent, wearily.

"What do you think *you* ought to do?" countered the senior evaluator.

The superintendent looked askance at the community education director in search of some kind of ready-made answer. What he found instead was an expression as enigmatic as his own. It just didn't make sense to either of them, thought the superintendent. Yet it was crystal clear to the university team.

"Who's right," he kept asking himself, "a participant or a program evaluator?" While he deliberated upon a best answer, he heard another member of the team say, "We're here to help you!"

## QUESTIONS

1. List the elements of Mavis' community education project. What areas, if any, were missing in it?

2. How adequate were Mavis' preparations for the evaluation team's visit?

3. Why was the evaluating team uninterested in Mavis' intinerary? How would site visits have helped the team members in their evaluation of the project?

4. What is your reaction to the position of the evaluating team?

5. How did Mavis' project reach its current success level without long-range goals or objectives?

6. What might be several long-range goals for a community education project?

7. What might be several short-range goals for a community education project?

8. On what basis had Mavis' project been termed successful?

9. "If you don't know where you're going, how will you ever know when you've arrived," stated the senior evaluator. Defend his statement.

10. Who is right — "participant or a program evaluator"? Elaborate.

## ACTIVITIES

1.  List the elements of Mavis' program on the blackboard. As a class effort, rate the programmatic efforts of the project. What elements are missing? How does this project compare with a model project?

2.  Role play the director concluding his report to the evaluation team. In what other ways might the team have reacted?

3.  In small groups, design goals and objectives for a community education project. As a whole-class activity, reach a consensus on goals and objectives. Field test the developed goals with practicing community educators.

4.  Through individual assignments, review the literature on goals for community education.

5.  As a class project, assist a community that is interested in initiating community education and develop goals unique to that community.

CASE #23

## MY DREAM IS YOURS

Parker Hayworth was positively delighted when he received an invitation to participate in a seminar for community education doctoral fellows at the university center for community education. As the coordinator of an extremely successful community education project, he was not unaccustomed to addressing both small and large groups three or four times a month, not only in his own school district, but also in other districts. Indeed, because of his inspirational speeches, many community education projects had come into existence. Never, however, had he been asked to speak at a university. Furthermore, the invitation had identified him, not as just a typical speaker, but as the key speaker.

Driving down to Waterbury University, the day before the seminar began, he was barely able to control his excitement. Accompanying him was one of his two community education directors, George Petersen, whom he had hired only recently because of program growth.

Petersen was greatly relieved when it was his turn to drive. The second hundred miles, he mused, would be a lot easier on his equanimity than the first.

Sprawling out on the back seat, Hayworth dozed off in seconds. The sleepless night he had experienced was exacting its toll from his gaunt frame.

At ten o'clock at night, they arrived in Waterbury and checked into a motel a few blocks from the university. After a light meal at a small but attractive restaurant, they hurried back to the motel to bed down for the night. Hayworth, ordinarily a night person, was asleep by eleven-thirty. By then Petersen had already begun to snore.

The next day promised to be productive. There were approximately thirty-five people assembled in the small auditorium when Hayworth entered. Standing behind the podium, he watched a few stragglers trail in. At ten minutes past nine Hayworth began his address.

"I'm happy to see so many potential community education leaders in my midst. And it's a rare pleasure to bring to you the Garlinden School District community education story. For I know whatever I say will be put to its best use." Hayworth's hands clutched the edges of the podium as he shifted the weight of his lean body from his right to his left foot.

"We began with a great deal of enthusiasm and very little community support five years ago. Our urban community was quick to classify community education as just another educational frill. For a while negativism ran rampant; then, slowly but surely, people started to get involved in the project. Today, we have hundreds of people participating in over a dozen different programs." Hayworth paused to rearrange his notes. The murmurs he was picking up from several students in the back rows distracted him, extending his silence. When the noise subsided, Hayworth resumed his speech.

"We have programs for preschoolers, teenagers, and adults. There are hot lunches for the kids who can't afford them, youth clubs for adolescents, high school equivalency courses for dropouts, and an array of activities for senior citizens. We've tied into our community education network various service clubs, neighborhood organizations, municipal agencies, and industrial concerns." Hayworth paused again, this time to assess the effect of his last statement.

"The results are overwhelming." Hayworth pounded the podium with his fist. "Delinquency is down, vandalism has been reduced, the dropout rate has dramatically declined, and an appreciable number of our citizens, having been awarded their high school diplomas, are presently enrolled in college courses in our facility and at a nearby community college. Besides these rather obvious benefits, other dividends are also accruing. People are taking a greater interest in their neighborhoods. In formerly run-down sections of the city, there are freshly painted homes, uncluttered yards, and well-kept lawns. Where only a modicum of communication took place before between neighbors, people are getting together in block parties and neighborhood civic associations. Many, previously on relief rolls, now work regularly."

Hayworth's voice was booming.

"If you could have shared this experience with me — I mean, us — and have witnessed the spectacular transformation, I feel certain you would quickly concur that community education is capable of producing miracles in an age when faith is often in short supply."

Hayworth continued to speak for another fifteen minutes, explaining in more elaborate detail the nature of program offerings. When he concluded, he invited questions from the audience.

One of the students in the back row stood up.

"Mr. Hayworth, I can appreciate your position and the strong feelings associated with it. But can you document what you say about the effects of community education on your city? Unfortunately, most of what goes on in community education, aside from head counts and program availability, is purely subjective — emotional reactions that simply have no scientific undergirding." The student sat down.

"In answer to your question," responded Hayworth with a tremor in his voice, "may I simply repeat that I have witnessed the events I speak of with my own eyes over a period of five memorable years. Am I to believe that I have deceived myself?" He finished gruffly.

Another student stood up.

"But have you conducted any formal studies?" he smirked.

"Some rather crude ones," said Hayworth, wincing. "The reason we didn't go overboard on studies was that we felt we didn't need to prove the obvious. The best indicator of success is program growth through active community involvement. A program which attracts an ever-increasing number of participants is bound to be a good one."

Still standing, the same student asked, "In those minor studies that you have alluded to, what kind of instrumentation did you use?"

Before Hayworth could answer, he heard another voice say, "Could we hear more about those minor studies. I, for one, am interested in the areas the study addressed."

Hayworth couldn't believe what he was hearing. No one seemed to be concerned about the merits of community education, only the merits of measurements. He had told them a great story, and they had closed their minds to it. The situation was unreal to him, a veritable nightmare.

As he formulated his reply, he grew cold and indifferent. There was no point in letting his audience ruffle him. Soon, he would be on his way home, back to the real world of community education, where dreams, not nightmares, had a habit of coming true. Meanwhile, he was prepared to stand aloof.

## QUESTIONS

1. Hayworth was asked to speak at the Waterbury University because he had a successful community education project in operation. What items did Hayworth list to prove his project was successful?

2. Hayworth stated that certain educational and social problems had been reduced. Apparently he could not document any of his claims. How would you evaluate progress in the following areas: juvenile delinquency; vandalism; dropout rate; neighborhood improvement?

3. What are the pros and cons of subjective data? Were Hayworth's observations worthless?

4. What criteria should be used to measure the success of a community education project? Of what significance are factors such as growth and expansion?

5. Who is the most logical person to conduct research studies in a community education project, and why?

6. How should community education be evaluated?

## ACTIVITIES

1. Using the brainstorming technique, list the areas of concern for the evaluation of community education.

2. As a class activity, review the literature concerning research in community education. Prepare an annotated bibliography.

3. As a class activity, develop an instrument and poll twenty community education directors in the state to ascertain the following: What research is being conducted in their project; who is conducting the research; the attitude of the community educator toward research; needed areas of research.

4. Divide the class into four groups. Obtain evaluation models from four school districts. Critique each model. Report to the class.

5. Develop a time line for evaluating a community education project, paralleling the overall development of the project.

6. In small groups, develop a master plan of evaluation for a community education project. Report to the class to reach a consensus.

CASE #24

## A HELPING HAND

It was the second day of the national convention for community educators. The morning session had just concluded. Three men and one woman, all community education directors, lingered in their seats to exchange their reactions to the key issues of a panel discussion. In forming a small cluster, the foursome sat facing each other within an arm's length.

Two members were old friends. Anne Welch and Stacy Marlowe, coming from the same state, had attended many regional workshops together. Jack Purdom and Harry Willowby, novices in community education, came from opposite ends of the country. Having met only yesterday, they had struck up an acquaintance with Welch and Marlowe just before the session began.

The group seemed troubled by the theme of the panel. Anne Welch was the first to speak.

"The panel certainly zeroed in on the importance of evaluation." She folded her arms and frowned. "Apparently, the future of community education depends upon our ability to develop sophisticated evaluation techniques."

" . . . which means, of course," interrupted Purdom, "that we had better clarify our goals if we intend to continue functioning as community education directors."

"Just what are our goals?" queried Marlowe. "I know what mine are, but I'd like to get a consensus of opinion to make me feel better," he bantered. His attempt at humor was no match for the seriousness in his eyes.

"In view of what I heard this morning," said Willowby, casually, "I'd say that any goal — or goals — we care to agree upon better be supportable by a lot of hard data. Otherwise, we're in for real trouble. The heyday of subjectivity is long past," added Willowby, pompously.

"The emotions are dead!" announced Marlowe, sarcastically. "Long live the computer."

"I find that amusing," said Welch, letting her arms fall to the sides of her chair. "It reminds me of a funny story I heard the other day about the computer, or rather the gentleman who had access to one." Leaning backwards in her chair, she giggled. "It seems there was this superintendent who wanted his community education director to conduct a monumental survey, the initial one having been more incidental than planned. The purpose of the survey was to provide substantial direction for the program. The result was a twenty-page survey, which asked every conceivable question known to mankind. It was a beautiful survey. But when it was fed into the computer and both the superintendent and the community education director were able to ask myriads of questions, nobody was quite sure what could be done with the answers. For all I know, they may still be asking questions and piling up answers. Can you imagine a room inundated with computer printouts? That's not community education; that's community chaos." Welch's giggle turned into full laughter.

Responding to her story, Marlowe was unable to suppress a smile. "That's precisely what I'm most concerned about." Then, he spoke gravely. "I'm afraid that we're going to become overly enamored with goal setting and data collection and forget about our real purpose — helping people!"

"Since we seem to be in the mood for stories," said Marlowe, pensively, "I'd like to tell a very serious one. It dates back to my first year as a community educator."

There was a distant look in Marlowe's eyes. "In those days, my sole objective was to fill up classrooms. I was a head counter, concerned with programs, not people. People were simply a means to an end. My game was empire building; and, oh, how I enjoyed it. Then I met Mrs. Dawson, and community education was never the same to me!"

"Sounds like the beginning of a soap opera," yawned Willowby. Glancing at his watch, he said, derisively, "Why don't we continue this exhilarating conversation over lunch. I'm positively famished."

"Let's hear the story first," insisted Anne Welch. "My interest has been aroused."

"Look," said Marlowe, apologetically, "if you folks are hungry, don't let me keep you. I can save the story for another time."

"I agree with Anne," said Purdom. "Lunch can wait a little longer. Tell us more about Mrs. Dawson. I could use an inspiration." He grinned.

As Marlowe resumed his narrative, he saw Willowby yawn a second time.

"Mrs. Dawson came to register for a high school equivalency course, accompanied by two small children, who looked like a pair of chimney sweeps. She wore an ensemble that lit her up like a Christmas tree. Her hair was disheveled, and her make-up absurdly overdone. Instead of a mouth, she had a huge red blotch. Yet, despite her gaudy clothes and her glaring paint job, she was still attractive and, believe it or not, quite diffident. After I helped her register and she thanked me about five times, I forgot about her.

"The following week I was reminded of her again when I stumbled over one of her children in the corridor. He was sitting, curled up on the floor, outside his mother's classroom. His brother was just a short distance away, getting a drink of water. While the class was in session, I invited the youngsters to spend some time with me in my office. I bought them a couple of hot chocolates, and they talked endlessly about themselves, their mother, and, occasionally, their father, whom they hadn't seen for a long time. He was away on a business trip. When he came home, they hoped he would bring them a lot of toys since the few that they had were evidently broken beyond repair. Freddy, the oldest boy, was in the third grade; Danny, the youngest, was in the first. They both liked school and usually looked forward to it each day. The boys lived with their mother, who worked as a waitress in a restaurant three blocks from their apartment. What they especially enjoyed was eating in the restaurant and having their mother bring things to them that they liked, but never had at home. What they didn't like was being left alone at nights. Sometimes their mother had to work very late.

"When class was almost over, I took the boys back to the place where I found them. Waiting for me was their mother, looking pale and small. Class had been dismissed early, and she was searching for her children. It was, then, that I told Mrs. Dawson that her children couldn't come with her to class anymore. I was firm.

" 'But I can't leave them alone,' she had said in a tiny voice. 'They're so small, and they frighten so easily at night in our small apartment, whenever I'm gone.'

"Believe me, I'm sorry," I had said. "Nevertheless, I must ask that you make other arrangements."

" 'I can't afford a baby-sitter,' she had said, lowering her eyes. 'And I can't afford to give up class either. With a high school diploma I stand a chance of getting a job that pays more than a few tips. We have so little now.' She had begun to cry."

Standing up, Willowby grunted, "Can't we finish this at lunch? It's getting late, you know."

"Go, if you like," said Purdom. "We can catch up with you. Just tell us where you plan to lunch." Willowby sat down and pouted.

Marlowe stiffened as the past continued to loom up before him.

"I finally gave in. For the next three weeks, İ let the kids play in my office. The subsequent week I established a baby-sitting service with the help of several PTA mothers, and everyone began to benefit. It was a good idea, and I owed it to Mrs. Dawson, out of whose need it was created.

"Near the end of the course, Mrs. Dawson stopped coming. Feeling like a friend of the family and a bit of a Dutch uncle to the two boys, I took it upon myself to pay the Dawsons a visit. The two room apartment was like the aftermath of a hurricane; and the air was close and fetid. Mrs. Dawson had taken sick, and her boys were playing nursemaid. They had no phone so I couldn't call a doctor until I left, which was only minutes after my arrival. An hour later, I returned with a doctor and my wife Peggy, who began to put the place in order."

Marlowe's voice cracked. There were tears in his eyes. "To make a long story short," he said, turning his face away from his colleagues, "Mrs. Dawson finished out the term, passed a high school equivalency examination, and was the proud recipient of a high school diploma. For a while she stayed on with us, taking a few courses that offered college credit. Eventually, she went on to a community college and majored in accounting. Peggy and I attended her graduation.

"During this five-year period, many other things happened, too. She divorced the husband who had deserted her, got herself a fine job as a bookkeeper in an insurance company, moved to a larger apartment, which she keeps impeccably clean, and began going steady with a widowed accountant, whom, I suspect, she'll soon marry.

"Peg and I visit her often. Having no children of our own, we've taken a special interest in the Dawson boys. Whenever we do, I find it difficult to make myself believe that I am seeing the same woman that I first saw standing in the school corridor. The difference is incredible."

"Whew," said Anne Welch, stretching out her arms. "That's quite a story." Purdom nodded in agreement.

"I'm happy you agree," said Marlowe. "But how do you evaluate changes of this kind? And how many people besides Mrs. Dawson have benefited from community education in the same way? Do we have to keep files on everyone that has ever taken a course to prove that community education is doing the job it was meant to do?"

"What do we do?" said Purdom, arching his eyebrows.

"We go to lunch," grumbled Willowby, moving toward the door. "If we wait any longer, it'll be time for dinner."

## QUESTIONS

1. Welch made the statement, "The future of community education depends upon our ability to develop sophisticated evaluation techniques." Develop a rationale for or against this statement.

2. The statement was made, "We are enamored with goal setting and data collection and we forget about our real purpose — helping people." As stated, this is an either-or situation. How can a balance be established?

3. Describe the positions of the community education directors on evaluation.

4. A lengthy description of Mrs. Dawson's situation was narrated. Can community education be successfully evaluated in this manner?

5. What is the value of the case study technique in community education?

6. How can head count (participation) be employed to evaluate community education?

7. List factors that cannot usually be controlled in evaluating community education.

8. To what extent should attitudinal assessments of program participants be used to evaluate community education?

9. How much emphasis is evaluation currently receiving in the community education movement?

## ACTIVITIES

1. Outline a case similar to Mrs. Dawson's from your own experience. Report to the class.

2. In small groups, discuss Mrs. Dawson's value system. Why was she motivated while many others are not? Each group report to the class.

3. As a class activity, discuss the role of research and evaluation in community education.

4. Obtain participation records from a school community education project or from a Regional Community Education Center. In small groups, analyze the data over a three-year period. Resume

whole-class activities for reports on small group proceedings.

5. Using the same data as above, each group design an instrument that would have made the data more reliable if it had been employed.

## ANNOTATED READINGS

Fish, Thomas. "Community Education Evaluation Around the Nation," *Community Education Journal*, Volume V, No. 2, March/April 1975, (pp. 40-43). Three articles are included in this section. They are brief descriptions of processes and techniques for evaluation used around the country. The reports emphasize the process used, but do not provide a rationale for the process or the specific instruments used. The three evaluation options have been employed; thus they are not just theory.

Hammond, Robert L. "Establishing Priorities for Information and Design Specifications for Evaluating Community Education Programs," *Community Education Journal*, Volume V, No. 2, March/April 1975, (pp. 13-16). Hammond, a member of the Phi Delta Kappa National Study Committee on Evaluation, has written this article for community educators. The article's purpose provides a comprehensive and systematic approach to establishing alternatives for program analysis, behavioral criteria for making judgments about the program, and a model for designing the evaluation. Evaluation is described as a process for examining and assigning values to observations of behavior of populations in an environment created by the community education program. The author warns that since every sub-program of community education has its own unique requirements, each must be treated as a separate design problem.

Hickey, Howard W., and Van Voorhees, Curtis. *The Role of the School in Community Education*, Midland, Michigan: Pendell Publishing Company, 1969. Chapter XI, Research and Evaluation, written by Howard W. Hickey. The chapter discusses successful community education research as a means to determine the characteristics of a community education program. Evaluation is considered as a way of determining how effectively community education uses community resources to meet community needs.

King, Marilyn. "A Review of the Literature in Evaluation for the Community Educator," *Community Education Journal*, Volume V, No. 2, (pp. 50-52). The author lists seven books concerned with evaluation that are applicable to community education. No one model of evaluation applies in every situation; thus the purpose of the article is to make the community educator aware of alternatives for project assessment.

Martin, Gerald C. "Must We Evaluate?", *Community Education Journal*, Volume I, No. 1, February 1971, (pp. 10-11). A regional center director for community education describes the need for evaluation and comments on the resistance of community educators to evaluation. He briefly discusses steps of evaluation and suggests steps to consider for increasing the evaluation effort in community education.

Minzey, Jack, and LeTarte, Clyde E. *From Program to Process*, Midland, Michigan: Pendell Publishing Company, 1973, (pp. 241-262). The why and how of evaluating community education programs are explored in this chapter. In stressing behavioral objectives and sample goals, the authors provide objectives and methods of evaluating. Practical hints are offered to the novice evaluator, and ways of collecting data are discussed.

Seay, Maurice F., and Associates. *Community Education: A Developing Concept*, Midland, Michigan: Pendell Publishing Company, 1974, (pp. 207-231). Evaluation and accountability are two misunderstood, feared, and sometimes ignored words in the development of a community education program. In this chapter, the authors discuss who should evaluate, what should be evaluated, and when evaluation is necessary. The writing of goals is approached with the idea of incorporating good writing in evaluations. Illustrated are several evaluation models which are supplemented by reference materials.

Steele, Marilyn. "Citizen Participation in the Planning/Evaluation Process: Case Studies," *Community Education Journal*, Volume V, No. 2, (pp. 28-30). The contention is made that citizens should be involved in the planning, evaluation, review, and implementation of community education projects. In this way, citizens can design the process to improve the quality of their lives and their community. Actual cases of citizen involvement in planning/evaluation in Delaware and Michigan are described.

Stufflebeam, Daniel L. "Evaluation as a Community Education Process," *Community Education Journal*, Volume V, No. 2, March/April 1975, (pp. 7-11, 19). The author outlines a proposed conceptualization of evaluation by posing ten basic questions. These questions are discussed in relationship to a matrix which depicts the relationship between evaluation roles and classes of variables. Theoretical contributions of several authorities and the Phi Delta Kappa Study Committee on Evaluation are combined to build Stufflebeam's operational definition.

Van Voorhees, Curtis. "Community Education Needs Research for Survival," *Phi Delta Kappan*, Volume LIV, No. 3, November 1972, (pp. 203-205). The community education movement has accelerated mainly because it is manned by action-oriented persons. The author states when a choice must be made between time devoted to research and time devoted to action, the latter is always chosen by community educators. The article briefly describes current research efforts in community education and incorporates what might be done in the way of future research.

Whitt, Robert L. "Accountability, Commitment and the Community School," *Community Education Journal*, Volume I, No. 1, February 1971, (pp. 21-22, 54). Quoting from the Gallup Poll, the author states that 75 percent of the adult public approves of accountability. The article weaves the community education concept into such areas as decentralization, community control, commitment, and education outside the school to explore the theme of accountability.

Wood, George S., Jr. "The Evaluation Process: The Place to Start Is with the Groundwork," *Community Education Journal*, Volume V, No. 2, (pp. 17-19). According to the author, some people in education pick up the nearest questionnaire and use it without regard to whether it was designed to do the job that they are trying to do. He states that one instrument to evaluate all community education would be a veritable monstrosity. The theme of the article is laying the groundwork for evaluation. The author identifies eight areas of investigation prior to the beginning stage of an evaluation and discusses each briefly.

Wright, William J., and Anderson, Beverly L. "An Approach to Evaluating Community Education," *Community Education Journal*, Volume V, No. 2, (pp. 37-39). The purpose of the article, as stated by the authors, is to outline a general approach to the evaluation of a community education program. The authors conceptualize and discuss the evaluation problem in the terms of the "natural life cycle" of what is being evaluated. A full-page table of the stages in the evaluation of a community education program is included.